Key Words in Christianity

Ron Geaves

continuum

The Continuum International Publishing Group
The Tower Building, 11 York Road, London SE1 7NX
80 Maiden Lane, Suite 704, New York, NY 10038

www.continuumbooks.com

© Ron Geaves, 2006

British Library Cataloguing-in-Publication Data
A catalogue record for this book is available from the British Library

ISBN 0-8264-8047-0 (paperback)

Typeset by Free Range Book Design & Production Ltd
Printed on acid-free paper in Great Britain by

Contents

PREFACE

During the course of teaching a number of religions in four higher education institutions, one common feature has been the number of students who have expressed to me that they have experienced the mastering of religious terminology in so many unknown languages and also involving unfamiliar concepts to be the most daunting part of the module. In view of this, the *Key Words* series was created to provide a glossary of terms for five religions.

The religions have been chosen to reflect the main traditions that are studied both in school and at university in the English-speaking world. One glossary also contains the key specialist terminology used in the academic study of religion. It is hoped that the glossaries will prove to be useful and informative resources for anyone studying religion up to undergraduate level, but that they will also provide a fascinating pool of information for anyone interested in religious practice or belief, whether for the purpose of gaining qualifications or simply in the personal pursuit of knowledge. Each glossary therefore provides an exhaustive exploration of religious terminology in a way that is accessible but also provides an overall in-depth understanding of the religious tradition.

Although Christianity is now provided with its own separate book, even so the glossary's completion remains arbitrary, as each religion covered by the *Key Words* series commands a vast vocabulary that is a conceptual framework for viewing the world. This is especially true of Christianity, which is over 2,000 years old and represents considerable religious diversity and a genuine global reach. This development and spread mean that Christianity could be argued to encompass several world-views. Although Christianity does not provide the difficulty of knowing terms in other languages, it cannot be assumed that today's student in the secular West knows any more about the beliefs and practices of Christianity than they know about any other religion. My choice of terms has been determined by school and undergraduate curricula, and the length of each definition has been dictated by the fact that this is a glossary and not a specialist religious dictionary. Inevitably, however, some concepts and persons needed more than a short passage in order to clarify their significance and highlight their importance within the world of their respective religion.

Finally, I would like to thank Catherine Barnes, whose patience and support has been remarkable; Janet Joyce, who provided the original opportunity for this project to grow from its inception to completion; and Continuum for providing the means for the glossaries to appear in their various editions.

A

Abbess   The title given to the heads of certain orders of nuns, particularly those of the BENEDICTINE rule. The Benedictines make life appointments but other orders, such as the FRANCISCANS, hold regular elections and circulate the position amongst the sisters of the institution. There is also a marked difference in degrees of authority between the various orders. (*See also* ABBOT)

Abbot   The title given to the heads of certain orders of monks, particularly those of the BENEDICTINE rule. An abbot has far-reaching powers over the maintenance and control of his community. He is perceived as the father of his community and is generally elected for life by his brothers. Other orders who appoint an abbot may be more democratic. (*See also* ABBESS)

Abjuration   The act of renouncing a previously held conviction or loyalty to a person or institution, sometimes required when Christians move from one denomination to another. (*See also* APOSTASY)

Ablutions   The ritual washing of the fingers in holy water by the PRIEST before the EUCHARIST. (*See also* MASS)

Absolution   The formal forgiveness of sins, pronounced by a PRIEST in the name of Christ and given to those who are penitent. Absolution is required before participating in the MASS or EUCHARIST. Although Roman Catholics still perform personal confession, in which the individual asks for forgiveness after acknowledging specific sins directly to a priest separated by a grid or curtain, it is now more common for all the congregants at the Mass or Eucharist to make a communal liturgical confession and receive communal forgiveness. (*See also* PENANCE; SIN)

Abstinence   Usually associated with not eating certain kinds of food on various feast days. Traditionally Roman Catholics did not eat meat on Fridays. In the Eastern churches there are around 150 days of abstinence in the calendar. (*See also* GOOD FRIDAY)

Acts of the Apostles   The fifth book of the NEW TESTAMENT, which is a valuable source of information on the early church after the death and resurrection of Jesus Christ. It was probably written by LUKE, PAUL's physician and fellow traveller, who accompanied the APOSTLE on evangelical journeys. The overall tone and themes of the writing suggest that one intention was to convince the Roman authorities that Christianity was not a threat to imperial order. The book begins with Jesus' ascension and the receiving of the HOLY SPIRIT at PENTECOST which transformed the demoralized apostles. It then goes on to record the development of the church in Jerusalem, the martydom of STEPHEN, early missionary work to the Jewish communities around the Mediterranean and the first contact with GENTILES. The book details the events that led to the conversion of Paul and the final section deals with his missionary journeys, culminating in his house arrest in Rome.

Actual Sin   A SIN which results from a free decision of the will to perform an ungodly act, as opposed to ORIGINAL SIN.

AD   The abbreviated form of *Anno Domini* (Latin: in the year of our Lord), used in the Christian calendar, which begins from the approximate date of the birth of Jesus Christ. (*See also* BC)

Adam   In Christian theology Adam is the first human being, whose fall from the state of GRACE is inherited by all succeeding generations until the intercession of Christ. Adam most frequently occurs in the letters of St PAUL, where he is contrasted with Jesus Christ. Christ is sometimes

2

likened to Adam before the FALL and is called the 'second Adam'. The victory of Christ over death at the RESURRECTION counteracts the punishment for Adam's original disobedience and allows the possibility for human beings to be reconciled with God as they were meant to be in the Garden of EDEN before the fall. (*See also* EVE)

Advent   *Lit. coming.* The time set aside for spiritual preparation for CHRISTMAS that originated in the merging of Gallican and Roman traditions. It begins on the fourth Sunday before Christmas except in the Eastern churches where it starts 40 days before. Traditionally it used to be a time of periodic preparatory fasting which was known as St Martin's Lent. Today, many people maintain an Advent calendar which provides a day-to-day run-in to the festival period of Christmas. Church sermons in the period of Advent tend to focus on calls to REPENTANCE.

Adventists   Various Christian communities who believe that the second coming of Christ is imminent. The movement was started by William Miller (1782–1849), a Baptist farmer from New York, who declared that Christ would come again in 1843. Despite the failure of the predictions, a variety of Adventist movements continue to exist. (*See also* JEHOVAH'S WITNESSES; SEVENTH DAY ADVENTISTS)

Agape   The Greek term for divine love as opposed to worldly love, it can be directed towards God, Christ or fellow Christians. The term is also used in the NEW TESTAMENT for the communal meal partaken by the early Christians that developed into the EUCHARIST.

Agenda   A liturgical term used to describe matters of religious practice as opposed to DOCTRINE, particularly the prescribed forms of service. (*See also* EUCHARIST; LITURGY)

Aisle   Traditionally used to describe an extension of the NAVE or main part of the church where the congregation are seated. However, today it is more commonly used to describe the walkway through the centre of the nave that divides the main body of the church and leads up to the SANCTUARY and ALTAR.

Albigensis An heretical movement that was widespread in twelfth- and thirteenth-century southern France, particularly in the area now known as Languedoc. They were GNOSTIC in many of their doctrines, believing that Christ was an angel who neither suffered on the cross nor was resurrected. REDEMPTION was not in Christ's death and RESURRECTION but rather in the teachings. The community considered material things to be evil, lived an ascetic life and opposed marriage. They were violently suppressed by Pope Innocent III in the twelfth century and by the fourteenth century they were effectively eliminated. (*See also* CATHARS)

All Saints' Day Part of the Christian liturgical calendar, the feast day which celebrates the community of all Christian saints. It is observed on 1 November in the West but on the first Sunday after PENTECOST in the Eastern Churches. (*See also* ALL SOULS' DAY)

All Souls' Day A day in the Christian liturgical calendar, held on 2 November in the West, immediately following ALL SAINTS' DAY. It is the day of commemoration for all the faithful who have already departed from this world.

Alleluia *Lit. praise to God.* An expression of joy used in praise of God that occurs in the Bible and was adopted into Christian liturgical use. In the Middle Ages various musical forms were adopted for the chanting of alleluia.

Altar A table used to celebrate the EUCHARIST or Communion usually situated at the front of the church and at the eastern end. Traditionally it stands between the SANCTUARY and the NAVE. The practice of celebrating the Eucharist on an altar table goes back to the early custom of observing the rite on the graves of the faithful departed.

Amen *Lit. verily.* Used to indicate agreement at the end of prayers.

Anabaptists Various Protestant groups who refused to allow their children to be baptized, as they believed that the participant should make a public and personal proclamation of faith before undergoing

BAPTISM. In addition, they rejected participation in warfare and maintained communal ownership of property. They were persecuted by both Roman Catholics and mainstream Protestants who followed LUTHER, CALVIN or ZWINGLI. Some works of scholarship refer to them as 'radical Protestants' or the 'left-wing of the REFORMATION'. (*See also* SUBMERSION)

Anamnesis   The liturgical commemoration of the PASSION, RESUR-RECTION and ASCENSION of Christ contained in certain prayers recited at the EUCHARIST. It takes place when the bread and cup are accepted in remembrance of Christ's death and offered in thanksgiving. (*See also* ANAPHORA)

Anaphora   The central prayers recited at the EUCHARIST, also known as Eucharistic prayers, and which contain the CONSECRATION, the ANAMNESIS and the Communion.

Andrew, St   One of the original twelve APOSTLES of Jesus Christ. Formerly a follower of JOHN THE BAPTIST who introduced him to Jesus, Andrew then introduced his brother, PETER, to Christ. The two were fishermen from the town of Bethsaida on the banks of the Sea of Galilee. Andrew is last mentioned as being with the disciples at the ASCENSION and is believed to have been crucified at Achaia. He is the patron saint of Scotland.

Angel   A heavenly being who acts as a messenger between God and human beings. Angels also form part of the divine court around the throne of God. Usually represented as God's spokesmen or personal agents, angels are also mentioned as agents of destruction and judgement, protection and deliverance, and sometimes as warners. (*See also* ARCHANGELS; GABRIEL)

Anglican Communion   The large variety of denominations around the world which acknowledge the leadership of the Archbishop of Canterbury and whose origins are linked with the CHURCH OF ENGLAND. For 250 years after the REFORMATION, the Church of England was restricted to the State Church of England and the Episcopal Church in

Scotland. At the end of the eighteenth century, an Act of Parliament was passed allowing the consecration of BISHOPS to serve abroad. Bishoprics were gradually established throughout the British Empire and colonies, beginning with the Protestant Episcopal Church of the USA.

Anglicanism   The system of DOCTRINE and practice maintained by the denominations that form part of the ANGLICAN COMMUNION. Although rejecting the authority of the POPE in Rome, Anglicanism maintained the episcopal authority but did not acknowledge its divine origin. Ecclesiastical tradition was acknowledged during the first four centuries of Christian tradition but was limited by the right of direct appeal to Scripture. (*See also* CHURCH OF ENGLAND)

Anglo-Catholic   *See* HIGH CHURCH.

Antichrist   The term *antichristos* only appears once in the NEW TESTAMENT, in the letters of St JOHN. The epistle refers to the enemy or denier of Christ, who will appear as a personification of the forces of darkness in the last days. He will be finally defeated by the return of Christ in glory. However, the same epistle also seems to refer to an atmosphere or mood of antichrist in which society denies Christ and becomes unrighteous. Amongst contemporary Christians, some perceive the antichrist to be a force of evil, whilst others believe him to be a historical person who will materialize prior to Christ's second coming.

Antinomianism   The view that Christians are released from the need to observe any moral law by the intervention of GRACE. It was maintained by several early GNOSTIC groups and appeared in a variety of heretical sects such as the Beguines and Beghards in the fourteenth century. In its extreme forms it asserts that none of the externals of religion have to be followed, including sacramental grace and good works. It was partially reasserted by the PROTESTANT reformers, including LUTHER. (*See also* JUSTIFICATION)

Antiphon   Sentences generally taken from Scripture that are recited before and after the PSALMS in VESPERS. In the Eastern Church it refers to various chants that are sung by two choirs using alternate voices.

Antitrinitarianism   A variety of Christian positions which deny the validity of the DOCTRINE of the TRINITY. They include the declared heresies of ARIANISM, EBIONITES, Modalists, and in the present day, UNITARIANISM.

Apocalyptic Literature   Christian sacred texts which claim to reveal things which are normally hidden, or to foretell the future. The most important apocalyptic text is the Book of REVELATION, the final book in the NEW TESTAMENT. Early Christianity was influenced by the tradition of apocalyptic literature in the Jewish sacred writings, which believed that the age when the fulfilment of prophecy would take place was yet to come. These types of literature were also a part of the tradition of messianic expectations. Both Jesus and the early Christian writers were influenced by apocalyptic thought, but the New Testament modifies it to the extent that God's redemptive work has already begun through the birth and death of Jesus Christ, and will extend to the final days. All Christians are therefore living in an apocalyptic time.

Apocryphal New Testament   A relatively modern title describing a variety of early Christian epistles and gospels which were not included in the canon of Scripture. The most important are the Acts of PETER, PAUL, JOHN, ANDREW and THOMAS, probably written in the second century CE. They are partly derived from oral tradition, popular curiosity to know more about the life of Christ, and the views of various heretical GNOSTIC movements.

Apologetics   The defence and explanation of the Christian faith by intellectual reasoning. The persecution of Christians gave rise to a variety of texts written from the second century onwards. The period from 130 to 180 is known as the age of the APOLOGIST.

Apologist   The title given to early Christian writers (c. 120–220) who first began the task of defending and explaining their faith to outsiders through the application of reason. Foremost amongst them are Quadratus, Aristides, Justin Martyr and Theophilus of Antioch.

Although they were highly valued amongst Christians, there is no evidence to suggest that they influenced non-Christian opinion or the Roman authorities. (*See also* APOLOGETICS)

Apostasy   In Christian Scripture, apostasy is defined as rebellion against God incited by SATAN. In the early Church, apostasy was seen as a great threat and was taken to be the act of falling away or giving up the faith. From that period to the present day it is regarded as defection from the Christian faith. The Roman Catholic Church uses the term to describe someone who publicly leaves the tradition.

Apostle   In the NEW TESTAMENT 'apostle' is used to describe Jesus Christ as one sent by God and those who were dispatched as missionaries in the early Church. The title is usually given to the most prominent 12 DISCIPLES of Christ who were selected and taught by him and who were sent out to preach the gospel with the power to heal and exorcize. They were witnesses to the RESURRECTION and, with the exception of JUDAS ISCARIOT who betrayed Jesus and then hanged himself in remorse, were the backbone of the development of the early Church.

Apostles' Creed   A usual statement of faith used by the Western churches and repeated in church services. Falling into three main sections, it provides the essence of Christian belief concerning God, Jesus and the HOLY SPIRIT. It also contains brief information on the essential beliefs concerning judgement, RESURRECTION and the Church. It was universally introduced in the West during the reign of Charlemagne (d. 814). (*See also* CREED)

Apostolic See   *See* VATICAN.

Apostolic Succession   The belief that the priesthood of the Roman Catholic and Anglican Churches is a direct succession from the original APOSTLES through an unbroken line of BISHOPS and maintains its authority on this basis. Most Protestants deny the validity of the Apostolic succession, which is replaced with the ideal of the priesthood of all believers. It was commonly called upon by opponents of female ordination in the CHURCH OF ENGLAND as a justification for their position that women cannot be called to the priesthood. (*See also* PRIEST)

Aquinas, St Thomas (1225–1274) A Dominican monk, eminent theologian and philosopher who was one of the key thinkers of medieval Christianity. His main works were *Summa Contra Gentiles*, in which he developed arguments for missionaries to use against Muslims and Jews and *Summa Theologiae*, in which he elaborated aspects of Christian theology such as the 'Five ways' arguments for the rational proof of God, his discussion of the relationship between faith and reason and his use of analogy, which allowed God to be known through creation. (*See also* SCHOLASTICISM; THOMISM)

Archangels The highest level in the hierarchy of ANGELS and the only ones to be given names. Some sources maintain there are four, whilst others state that there are seven. The most commonly mentioned and well known are GABRIEL and Michael.

Archbishop A BISHOP who has authority over an ecclesiastical province which is made up of several DIOCESES. The highest cleric in the CHURCH OF ENGLAND is the Archbishop of Canterbury. (*See also* ARCHDIOCESE)

Archdeacon A priest in the ANGLICAN COMMUNION who has DIOCESAN administrative duties delegated to him from the BISHOP.

Archdiocese The DIOCESE or ecclesiastical territory under the jurisdiction of an archbishop. It contains several dioceses under the control of BISHOPS, which in turn are made up of parishes under the jurisdiction of a parish priest.

Arianism An influential DOCTRINE branded as HERESY which was not resolved until CONSTANTINE convened the Council of NICAEA in 325 to deal with disputes in the Empire. The doctrine denied that Christ was eternal or divine and asserted that he was only the principal or foremost of God's creatures, although unlike any other creature. He was created by the Father and therefore not God by nature. The

9

doctrine was asserted by Arius (250–336), a PRIEST of Alexandria, who, as a strict monotheist, emphasized the total transcendence and inaccessability of God to all creatures, including the Son. He was excommunicated at the Council of Alexandria and further condemned at NICAEA.

Armageddon   The site of the great battle that will be fought during the last days, according to the Book of REVELATION. It is the apocalyptic assembly point for the final struggle between the forces of good and the forces of evil. It is speculated that the geographical location is the plateau of Megiddo in Israel, the site of many battles throughout history. (*See also* PAROUSIA)

Ascension   The transporting of the risen Christ to heaven as witnessed by the APOSTLES 40 days after the RESURRECTION and recorded in the Gospel of LUKE and the ACTS OF THE APOSTLES. Although there are contemporary objections that heaven does not exist in a temporal direction, it is central to Christian belief that the physical manifestation of Christ departed from this world avoiding the normal human processes associated with death. Jesus has moved to a heavenly state and the HOLY SPIRIT replaces his presence on earth until the second coming when Christ will return to the earth in glory. (*See also* CRUCIFIXION)

Ash Wednesday   The first day of LENT that begins the forty days of abstention leading up to EASTER. A popular custom was to place ashes on the heads of the clergy and the congregation. Protestants ceased the practice after the REFORMATION although it remains a part of the Roman Catholic missal.

Athanasian Creed   A profession of faith once used in the Western churches but now only employed on certain special occasions by the Roman Catholic Church and rarely in Anglican churches. It contains the doctrines of the TRINITY and the INCARNATION and adds the most important events in Jesus' life. (*See also* CREED)

Atonement   The reconciliation or propitiation between God and human beings through the death and RESURRECTION of Jesus Christ, which atoned for the ORIGINAL SIN of ADAM. The Jewish Scriptures tell of the FALL from GRACE of the first human beings, Adam and EVE and their expulsion from the Garden of EDEN. Consequently, the human race is unable to deal with SIN and the separation from God. The essential message of the NEW TESTAMENT is that the sacrificial act of CRUCIFIXION by Jesus Christ atoned for the fallen condition of humanity.

Augustine of Hippo, St (354–430) The most influential Christian theologian and BISHOP of Hippo from 395. At the age of 32 he underwent a sudden conversion after reading St PAUL's Epistle to the Romans. His writings are substantial, especially his detailed expositions of St Paul, and were to form the basis of Christian theology in the early medieval period. He is most famously known for his formulation of the DOCTRINE of ORIGINAL SIN and PREDESTINATION, but also provided key contributions to the theological areas of the SACRAMENTS and the doctrines of GRACE and the TRINITY. It can be argued that Augustine was the forerunner of the academic study of theology.

Authorized Version The 1611 English edition of the Bible authorized by King James I and often known as the 'King James version'. It replaced the GENEVA BIBLE published in Switzerland by Protestant exiles from the reign of the Catholic Queen Mary. For generations it remained the official Bible for the English-speaking world and is still used by many Protestant sects.

B

Banns   The traditional custom of announcing coming marriages in church services, normally three Sundays before the actual wedding. (*See also* SACRAMENT)

Baptism   The sacramental rite of initiation into Christianity which involves immersion into, or sprinkling with water. The rite is regarded as purification by washing away past sins and as regenerative, as one enters the Christian communion reborn in the life of the spirit. The custom goes back to the mission of JOHN THE BAPTIST and the baptism of Jesus. The earliest converts to the new faith were baptized and PAUL acknowledges that baptism was the initiation rite for the first Christians. There have been strenuous debates in Christianity concerning infant baptism. Although there are no direct references to infant baptism in the NEW TESTAMENT, there are passages indicating that entire households were baptized. The more that baptism is perceived as an expression of faith, the more likely it is that the Christian denomination or movement will oppose infant baptism. However, if baptism is seen as an expression of GRACE and forgiveness of ORIGINAL SIN, then infant baptism becomes justifiable. Where infant baptism is practised, there is normally a CONFIRMATION rite at puberty, which allows the initiate to make a conscious statement of faith. In many Christian nations baptism is sought by parents as a rite of passage and naming ceremony for newborn children without any meaningful consideration of the religious implication. (*See also* ANABAPTISTS; BAPTISTS; BELIEVER'S BAPTISM; SUBMERSION)

Baptistry   A building or a pool used for BAPTISM or a place in a church where baptism takes place. The spread of the popularity of infant baptism led to the establishment of FONTS, traditionally placed at the west end of the church or at the opposite end of the NAVE to the SANCTUARY.

Baptists   A Protestant denomination founded in the sixteenth century and influenced by the ideas of the ANABAPTISTS, they are widespread in the USA. Their name derives from the conviction of an early founder, John Smyth (1570–1612), who established the English Baptists, that the APOSTLES admitted new members to the Christian community through BAPTISM involving profession of REPENTANCE and acceptance of Jesus Christ. This conviction that baptism should be the rite of initiation for believers only means that they do not advocate infant baptism. Consequently only adults are baptized by the means of total immersion into water. (*See also* BELIEVER'S BAPTISM; SUBMERSION)

Barabbas   A robber or bandit who had been involved in some kind of homicidal incident (possibly linked with Jewish political aspirations), who was released instead of Christ by PONTIUS PILATE. As was the custom on the feast of Passover, Pilate had offered the Jews the choice of freeing one prisoner, in this case either Jesus Christ or Barabbas. (*See also* CRUCIFIXION)

Barnabas, St   One of the earliest DISCIPLES in Jerusalem amongst those converted after the death of Jesus Christ. He is mentioned in the NEW TESTAMENT for selling his property for the good of the Church, and PAUL describes him as an APOSTLE. After his conversion experience on the road to Damascus, Barnabus introduced him to the apostles in Jerusalem and later travelled with him on some of his missionary journeys. He was active in the debates that took place between Paul and the Church in Jerusalem regarding Jewish customs being applicable to GENTILE converts. Barnabus is regarded as the founder of the Church of Cyprus.

Bartholomew, St   One of the original twelve APOSTLES who were chosen by Jesus Christ as his companions and missionaries. Although mentioned in all the NEW TESTAMENT lists of the original twelve, nothing further is said about him.

Basilica   An early CHURCH design based on Roman architecture. In Roman Catholicism, the title of basilica is given as a sign of privilege by the POPE to certain churches.

BC   The term used in the Christian calendar to refer to the period of history that precedes the birth of Christ. (*See also* AD)

Beatific Vision   The state of union with, or the vision of, God in paradise which is regarded as the final destination of the saved. It is the ultimate goal of human existence and some DENOMINATIONS believe that it can be bestowed on exceptional individuals for brief moments in their lives. (*See also* HEAVEN; SAINT)

Beatification   A Roman Catholic practice whereby the POPE allows public veneration of a faithful Catholic after his/her death. It is the required stage before CANONIZATION, or the conferring of sainthood. The beatified person is given the title of 'blessed'. (*See also* SAINT)

Beatitudes   The qualities of perfection as described by Christ in his SERMON ON THE MOUNT and the foundation of Christian ethics. They are described in Matthew's Gospel (5.3–10) as a series of blessings as follows:
Blessed are the poor in spirit, for theirs is the kingdom of heaven.
Blessed are those who mourn, for they will be comforted.
Blessed are the meek for they will inherit the earth.
Blessed are those who hunger and thirst for righteousness, for they will be filled.
Blessed are the merciful, for they will be shown mercy.
Blessed are the pure in heart, for they will see God.
Blessed are the peacemakers, for they will be called sons of God.
Blessed are those who are persecuted because of righteousness, for theirs is the kingdom of heaven.

Beelzebub   In the OLD TESTAMENT, Beelzebub (Baal-Zabub) is the name given to an Ekron deity supplicated by Ahaziah, a king of Israel, as he lay dying from an incurable illness. However, in the NEW TESTAMENT, the name is given to the prince of devils and associated with SATAN.

Believer's baptism   The term used to refer to BAPTISM of adults who are old enough to experience and understand the Christian commitment involved, as opposed to the baptism of infants (*See also* ANABAPTISTS; BAPTISTS; SUBMERSION).

Benedicamus   A formula meaning 'let us bless the Lord' used in the conclusion of some of the OFFICES. (*See also* VESPERS)

Benedict, St   (480–550). Known as Benedict of Nursia and the founder of the BENEDICTINE monastic rule, he withdrew from the world to live as a hermit in a cave near Subiaco in Italy. However, he attracted followers and organized them into small communities around him. He established 12 MONASTERIES, each with 12 MONKS under the authority of an ABBOT. Benedict moved to Monte Cassino, between Rome and Naples, where he founded the monastery upon which the Bendictine Order is based.

Benedictine   The monastic order founded by St BENEDICT, based upon his *Rule*. Arguably the most influential of the monastic orders, it provided the norm for Western monastic traditions. There is great stress placed upon scholarship and learning, and the *Rule* itself is noted for its detail. Benedict's vision of monastic life was of a self-supporting community dedicated to following Christ, made up of lifetime members who were committed to celibacy and non-ownership. The head of the community is an ABBOT who must be obeyed. The principal activities of the MONKS are communal praise of God through the divine offices, manual labour in the MONASTERY and meditative study of the Scripture. The order grew slowly in spite of the patronage of Pope Gregory the Great but by the Middle Ages, its monasteries were the most important learning centres in Europe. (*See also* OFFICE; RELIGIOUS)

Benediction A blessing that offers to the individual or the congregation the favour of God. It is given by a PRIEST and conferred at various points in Christian LITURGY, most notably at the blessing of the elements at CONSECRATION. It is customary to provide a blessing at the end of worship.

Benedictus A song of thanksgiving taken from the Gospel of LUKE (1.68–79), originally attributed to ZACHARIAH on the birth of his son, JOHN THE BAPTIST. In the Western Church it is sung in MATINS.

Bethlehem The reputed birthplace of Christ 5 miles south of JERUSALEM, associated in Jewish prophecy as the birthplace of the MESSIAH, as it was also the native city of DAVID and the home of his ancestors. The city is famous for the pilgrimage gathering that takes place at CHRISTMAS, when Christians gather at the Church of the Nativity erected by Helena in the reign of CONSTANTINE and proclaimed to be the birthplace of Jesus Christ.

Bible The Christian collection of sacred writings consisting of the OLD TESTAMENT and NEW TESTAMENT that are considered to be canonical. The Old Testament consists of the Jewish Scriptures and the New Testament consists of the GOSPELS that recount the birth, life, death and teachings of Jesus Christ, and the books that tell of the development of the early Church. (*See also* EPISTLES)

Binitarianism The doctrine that opposes the orthodox theology of the TRINITY and asserts that there are only two persons in the Godhead, the Father and the Son. (*See also* UNITARIANISM)

Bishop The highest order of MINISTERS or PRIESTS in the Episcopalian churches. Although the origin of bishops has been disputed, certainly by the second century they seem to have been in control of all the main centres of Christianity and remained unchallenged until the REFORMATION. The authority of Roman Catholic and Anglican bishops is based upon APOSTOLIC SUCCESSION but some Protestant Churches have retained bishops without subscribing to this DOCTRINE. Today, the principal duties of a bishop are the performance of SACRAMENTS and the administration of a DIOCESE, or ecclesiastical territory consisting of several parishes. In Catholicism, bishops are distinguished from other priests in that they confer holy orders and administer CONFIR-MATION.

Black Theology A movement begun in the 1960s in the USA to ensure that black Christians and their experience of Christian life was represented in theology. Originally arising out of the civil rights movement and as a reaction against white domination in Western Christianity, it began in the Black Protestant communities of North America and stressed suffering and the importance of liberation. This focus led to a wider identification with LIBERATION THEOLOGY and the development of black-led churches.

Blackfriars A popular name for the MONKS of the DOMINICAN order which arises from the black cowls they wear over their white habits.

Blessed sacrament A name sometimes used for the EUCHARIST rite but more commonly applied to the bread and wine which has been consecrated for the Eucharist SACRAMENT.

Breviary A liturgical book which contains the PSALMS, HYMNS and LESSONS used by the Roman Catholic Church for divine OFFICES. However, since VATICAN COUNCIL II, offices are no longer a daily requirement of PRIESTS and are mostly confined to monastic orders.

C

Caiaphas The Jewish high priest from 18 to 36 CE who presided over the trial of Jesus Christ and the persecutions of the early Christians described in the ACTS OF THE APOSTLES. (*See also* CRUCIFIXION)

Calvary The reputed place of Christ's CRUCIFIXION described in the GOSPELS as being outside JERUSALEM near a garden containing a tomb. Today there are two locations believed to be the site of Calvary, also known as Golgotha ('the place of skulls'). One is the Church of the HOLY SEPULCHRE and the other is the Garden Tomb, also known as Gordon's Calvary.

Calvin, John (1509–64) A French Protestant reformer who broke with the Roman Catholic Church after receiving a vision in which he believed that God instructed him to transform the Church to its original purity. In 1541, he returned to Geneva, where he had initially fled on breaking with Rome, and established a theocratic state which placed the government in the hands of the clergy. The state inflicted harsh penalties for breaches of religious discipline and all opposition was overcome by force. (*See also* CALVINISM; REFORMATION)

Calvinism The Protestant theological system developed by John Calvin (1509–64) and part of the REFORMATION. Calvinism differs from LUTHERANISM in that it did not intend to challenge the DOCTRINE of the church but only to change worship and moral laws so that they conformed to Scripture. However, Calvinism emphasizes PREDESTINATION, ELECTION and ORIGINAL SIN. Aspects of Calvinism are accepted by BAPTISTS, PRESBYTERIANS and the REFORMED CHURCHES of France, Switzerland and Holland. Because other thinkers besides Calvin have influenced the developments of these traditions, they prefer to be known as Reformed Christianity. (*See also* PURITANS)

Candlemas   A feast day in the Christian liturgical calendar, on 2 February, which celebrates the purification of the Virgin MARY and Christ's presentation at the Temple. It is known as Candlemas because of the Roman Catholic tradition of processing with lighted candles.

Canon   The title given to members of the secular CLERGY who are on the staff of a CATHEDRAL or collegiate church, either as full-time salaried staff responsible for the maintenance of its ecclesiastical functions or as unsalaried volunteers.

Canon Law   The complete collection of ecclesiastical rules which govern matters of DOCTRINE, morals and discipline. The main body of canon law has been derived from the decisions made at a number of COUNCILS throughout the history of Christianity.

Canon of Scripture   The authoritive collection of Scripture in Christianity, made up from the accepted books of the OLD TESTAMENT and NEW TESTAMENT. The main texts were fixed in the Patristic period but they vary slightly from DENOMINATION to denomination. Although there was discussion over the Epistle to the HEBREWS, REVELATION, and the EPISTLES of Peter, John and Jude, the final CANON of Scripture was agreed by the beginning of the fifth century. (*See also* APOCRYPHA; BIBLE)

Canonization   The conferral of sainthood on a dead member of the Church, declared by the POPE in Roman Catholicism or a synod of BISHOPS in Eastern Orthodoxy. Originally the declaration of sainthood was made at diocesan level, but the problems brought about by the lack of central control led to papal intervention. (*See also* BEATIFI-CATION; SAINT)

Canterbury   Since the fourteenth century, Canterbury Cathedral has been the foremost SEE in England and after the REFORMATION continued the same function for the ANGLICAN COMMUNION. The first church in the UK was established by St Augustine of Canterbury, who was sent from Rome to England as a missionary in 597. The Archbishop of Canterbury is the PRIMATE of all England and effective leader of the State Church. (*See also* CHURCH OF ENGLAND)

Canticle A song or prayer derived from the Bible which is used in Christian worship. The most important are the MAGNIFICAT, NUNC DIMITTIS and the BENEDICTUS, which are used in the daily divine OFFICES.

Capernaum A town on the north-west shore of the Sea of GALILEE close to the River JORDAN which became the headquarters of Christ during his Galilean ministry. The house of the disciple PETER was in Capernaum and there are accounts of it being visited by pilgrims up until the fourth century. By the sixth century it had been replaced by a basilica.

Capuchins An important new religious order founded in Italy in the sixteenth century by Matteo de Bascio (1495–1552) and three companions. They were all FRANCISCANS determined to restore the order to its original intention by following to the letter the *Rule* of St FRANCIS. The Capuchins are known for their distinctive course habit and four-pointed hood (cappuchio), from which they derive their name.

Cardinal The title conferred on PRIESTS usually with the rank of BISHOP, who form the COLLEGE of immediate counsellors to the POPE. Their function is essentially administrative and they reside in the VATICAN unless bishops of a foreign DIOCESE. Since 1179 they have held the privilege of electing the Pope. (*See also* ROMAN CATHOLIC)

Carmelites A mendicant ORDER, properly called the Order of Friars of the Blessed Virgin Mary of Mount Carmel but also known as the White Friars, that was founded in 1154 by Berthold of Calabria, who established a community of hermits that were renowned for their extreme asceticism and mysticism. In 1238, they left the Holy Land for Europe and ceased to be hermits, organizing themselves in urban cloisters. The MONKS and NUNS are renowned for their ardent devotion to the Virgin MARY. (*See also* DOMINICANS; FRANCISCANS; FRIARS; RELIGIOUS)

Carol   A song of joy that celebrates the nativity or birth of Jesus Christ, usually sung at the festival of CHRISTMAS.

Carthusians   A silent ORDER of solitary contemplative MONKS, founded by St Bruno of Cologne. Having withdrawn from the world to join a number of hermits near Grenoble, in 1084 he founded a MONASTERY that attempted to combine monastic and hermit lifestyles. The monks lived as hermits undertaking vows of silence, but came together for worship and mealtimes. (*See also* RELIGIOUS)

Cassock   The long gown, usually black, which is the standard wear of Christian clergy. In the Roman Catholic Church, BISHOPS wear purple, CARDINALS wear red and only the POPE is garbed in white. (*See also* VESTMENTS)

Catacombs   Underground burial places used by early Christians as places of refuge during persecution. Since Roman law regarded cemeteries as sacrosanct, Christians could use them for hiding and the performance of the EUCHARIST with little possibility of discovery. The most extensive catacombs are in Rome. (*See also* MARTYR)

Catechism   The manual of Christian DOCTRINE in a question-and-answer format, generally associated with teaching those preparing for CONFIRMATION.

Catechumens   The name given in the early Church to those awaiting BAPTISM and undergoing the necessary preparations. The Roman Catholic Church restored the Catechumate in 1972 for adult baptisms.

Cathars   A rigidly dualistic Christian sect branded as HERESY. It spread throughout Germany and Italy in the twelfth century but was best known in the South of France where it was named ALBIGENSIS.

Cathedra   The throne of a BISHOP maintained in his respective CATHEDRAL, which both demonstrates his ecclesiastical authority in the DIOCESE and symbolizes his position in the lineage of APOSTOLIC SUCCESSION.

Cathedral   A church containing the BISHOP's throne, usually larger and more splendid than a normal parish church. The activities of the DIOCESE, extending over several parishes, will be coordinated by the cathedral staff.

Catholic   First and foremost, it refers to the full or universal Christian community regardless of any DENOMINATIONAL loyalty. It is also used as a popular abbreviation for the ROMAN CATHOLIC Church. More uncommonly it refers to Christianity before the schism into Eastern and Western Churches.

Celtic Church   The church which already existed in Britain before the arrival of Roman Christianity in 597. There are accounts of BISHOPS representing British Christianity at the Council of Arles in 314. After the invasion of the Saxons, British Christians took shelter in Wales, Scotland and Cornwall. These communities, together with Irish Christianity, became known as Celtic. Celtic Christianity had a very strong monastic and hermit tradition and pursued a particularly zealous missionary role. There were theological, political and organizational differences between the Celtic and the Roman Churches. At the Council of Whitby in 664, the two traditions presented their views, but King Oswy declared loyalty to Rome when he learned that the POPE in Rome was the direct successor of the APOSTLE Peter. In the latter part of the twentieth century there was a strong attempt to revive the spirituality of Celtic Christianity in Britain.

Chalcedonian Declaration   The declaration made at the fourth ecumenical council in 451 that confirmed the decisions of the Council of NICAEA concerning the divinity and humanity of Jesus Christ. The declaration stated that Jesus was both fully human and fully divine. (*See also* ARIANISM; CHRISTOLOGY)

Chalice   A long-stemmed cup, usually silver, although early versions were made of glass, which contains the wine for use in the EUCHARIST.

Chancel   The area of a church that used to be known as the SANCTUARY but now also includes the area reserved for the choir and the PRIEST, as well as the area surrounding the ALTAR.

Chantry   A chapel in a church which is reserved for prayers for the soul of the founder, and for his friends or family to celebrate MASS. Chantries were as common as independent CHAPELS until the REFORMATION and the Chantry PRIEST often acted in the capacity of local schoolteacher.

Chapel   A smaller place of worship contained within a church or CATHEDRAL, or a small room or hall used for prayer in a school, hospital, college or private home. It is also used to describe the places of worship which belong to dissenting Protestant DENOMINATIONS separate from the CHURCH OF ENGLAND. (*See also* NON-CONFORMISTS)

Chaplain   A member of the CLERGY who does not have parish duties but works in public institutions such as hospitals, universities, prisons and schools, taking care of the pastoral needs of the residents.

Chapter   The members of the governing body responsible for an ecclesiastical institution such as a CATHEDRAL. (*See also* CANON)

Charismatic   A contemporary movement influenced by EVANGELICALISM, and particularly PENTECOSTALISM, which has spread across DENOMINATIONS. Charismatics place particular emphasis on the presence and experience of the HOLY SPIRIT. Although conservative in its theology and interpretation of Scripture, it is spontaneous in forms of worship. Charismatics emphasize religious experience such as being 'born again in the spirit', healing, or speaking in tongues.

Chrism   A mixture of olive oil and balsam used for anointing (chrismation) in the SACRAMENTS of BAPTISM, CONFIRMATION, ORDINATION and the dedication of sacred buildings within the Greek ORTHODOX

CHURCH and Roman Catholic church. It is usually consecrated on MAUNDY THURSDAY by either a BISHOP or a PATRIARCH. It is kept in a container known as the Chrismata.

Chrismata   *See* CHRISM.

Chrismation   *See* CHRISM.

Christ   *Lit. the anointed one.* The Greek translation of the Jewish word for MESSIAH. The Jewish tradition expected a leader who would herald God's salvation. The DISCIPLES of Jesus gave him the title, especially after his RESURRECTION, and it has come to refer to the divine nature of the resurrected figure as opposed to the human figure of Jesus of Nazareth. (*See also* CHRISTIANS; JESUS CHRIST)

Christian   The name given to the followers of JESUS CHRIST regardless of DENOMINATIONAL loyalty and also used in a nominal sense to describe the indigenous populations of secular nations that are historically Christian. The Book of Acts in the NEW TESTAMENT places the first use of the term 'Christian' as a self-ascription to the followers of Christ in Antioch. However, it is likely that the term was first used as a nickname by outsiders to describe the followers of the new religion and then became adopted by the followers themselves. (*See also* CHRIST)

Christmas   The festival which celebrates the nativity of Christ held in the Western Churches on 25 December. It is not actually known when Jesus Christ was born and it is speculated that the festival, which was certainly held on this date as early as 331, was originally the pagan solstice festival. On midnight of Christmas Eve there is a traditional candlelit EUCHARIST. The twelve days of the Christmas period also contain the holy days of St STEPHEN (26 December), St JOHN (27 December), Holy Innocents (28 December), The Circumcision of Our Lord (1 January) and EPIPHANY (6 January). In the Christian world, New Year is marked on 1 January. (*See also* NICHOLAS, ST)

Christology   Christian theology which deals with the significance, identity and nature of CHRIST. Much of the debate takes place around theories concerning the relationship between Christ and God and the nature of the balance between the human and divine nature of Jesus Christ. (*See also* ARIANISM; CHALCEDONIAN DECLARATION; DOCETISM; EBIONITES; NICAEA, COUNCIL OF)

Church   A term used to variously to describe the community consisting of all Christians, a particular DENOMINATION of Christianity and an individual Christian place of worship. The word is derived from the Greek 'the Lord's House' but the NEW TESTAMENT uses the word *ekklesia* which means a community or local congregation of Christian worshippers and has no connotation of a building. However, the New Testament also refers to the Church as the new society created by Christ as the participant of the new covenant to replace Israel. The Roman Catholic church focuses attention on participation in the SACRAMENTS as defining the Church, but Protestant groups have changed the emphasis to participation in the word of God. Questions of Christian unity have led to a distinction between the visible church, which is a human manifestation prone to error and correction, and the invisible church which is the body of the saved known only to God. (*See also* CATHEDRALS; CHAPELS)

Church of England   That part of the ANGLICAN COMMUNION which formally exists as the state religion of Britain. It came into existence during the REFORMATION when Henry VIII split from Rome after the POPE refused to annul his marriage. Henry was acknowledged as the supreme head on Earth of the Church of England, since when it has recognized the reigning monarch as its temporal leader. Although it does not acknowledge the Pope, many aspects of the Church of England remain essentially Catholic, including EPISCOPACY and belief in the authority of tradition as well as Scripture and acknowledgement of the APOSTOLIC SUCCESSION. The Catholic wing of the Church was rejuvenated by the OXFORD MOVEMENT, and the Church today perceives itself as a broad and tolerant alliance of HIGH CHURCH and LOW CHURCH, Anglo-Catholics, EVANGELICALS and CHARISMATICS. Since the second half of the twentieth century, it has become more autonomous from the state and the issue of disestablishment is prominent. (*See also* CANTERBURY; COMMON PRAYER, THE BOOK OF; THIRTY-NINE ARTICLES)

Church Militant, The   The body of Christians who still remain living on Earth as human beings rather than those already departed to PURGATORY or HEAVEN. The term suggests that they are still engaged in the struggle between the forces of good and evil. (*See also* SATAN; SIN)

Churchwardens   In the CHURCH OF ENGLAND they are members of the laity elected to be responsible for the objects and furniture in the church building.

Churchyard   The land in which a church stands but which is often used to describe the burial ground maintained in the precincts of a church.

Cistercians   The monastic order founded in France in 1098 by Robert, ABBOT of the MONASTERY at Molesme, and a small band of companions. They established a new monastery at Citeaux, also known as Cistercium, based on a life of great strictness. It originated as an attempt to reform the BENEDICTINES on the basis of strictness and simplicity and return to the original observance of the Benedictine rule. The MONKS are known as 'White Monks' because of their simple garb of undyed wool. The order spread under the influence of St Bernard of Clairvaux (1090–1153) during the twelfth century.

Clare, St   (1194–1253) A friend and disciple of St FRANCIS OF ASSISI, who joined him in 1212 and was established with a few companions in the MONASTERY founded by St Francis in the church of St Damion in the city. She developed it into the women's branch of the FRANCISCAN order, which is called the Poor Clares after her.

Clergy   The body of all persons ordained for religious service or to conduct the services of any Christian church. Individual members of the clergy range according to the various hierarchies existing in different DENOMINATIONS, but in general can be divided between those who belong to the category of PRIEST, a representative of God to the people with supernatural functions mostly relating to the celebration of the EUCHARIST, and those who are called to minister or perform spiritual functions within the Protestant churches. (*See also* ARCHBISHOP; BISHOP; CARDINAL; DEACON; DEAN; VICAR)

Cloister   The enclosed space at the centre of a MONASTERY or other religious building. It is sometimes used to describe a monastery itself or the life of a RELIGIOUS enclosed within one of the monastic orders.

Coenobite   A MONK or a NUN who lives in a monastic community as opposed to the solitary life of a hermit. (*See also* RELIGIOUS)

Collect   Short prayers used in the EUCHARIST which consist of an invocation and petition in Christ's name.

College   The assembly of CARDINALS in Roman Catholicism which acts as an advisory body to the POPE and gathers after his death to select a new pontiff. (*See also* CONCLAVE)

Colossians, Epistle to the   A short EPISTLE contained in the NEW TESTAMENT, attributed to PAUL but its authorship has been challenged on linguistic and doctrinal grounds. It is written to the Christian community in Colossae after Paul had received news that they were under threat from false teachers that were leading people away from the message preached by Christ. The author does not refute the heresies but lays out a clear position of correct Christian teaching.

Comforter   *See* HOLY SPIRIT.

Common Prayer, The Book of   The official service book of the CHURCH OF ENGLAND compiled in 1549 by Archbishop Cranmer, and which contains the order of service for morning and evening prayer and the SACRAMENTS. The Book of Common Prayer has gone through many revisions outside England, but the Church of England has generally maintained the original 1662 version. However, new books of alternative services were produced in the twentieth century.

Communion   *See* EUCHARIST.

Communion Table   *See* ALTAR.

Compline   In the Western Church, the final OFFICE said before sleeping. It consists of a HYMN, PSALMS and the NUNC DIMITTIS. Although maintained in monastic communities, in the Anglican churches it has been combined with VESPERS and incorporated into EVENSONG.

Comprecation   The intercession of the SAINTS made to God on behalf of all other Christians. Rejected by Protestant traditions, it remains an important part of Roman Catholic belief and common practice.

Conclave   The gathering of Roman Catholic CARDINALS that takes place within an enclosed room at the VATICAN, known as the Conclave, in order to select a new POPE from amongst their number after the death of the present incumbent.

Confession   The term confession is used in different ways in Christianity. The first simply implies an admission of SIN by a Christian. However, several DENOMINATIONS provide the possibility for personal confession to a PRIEST as well as the general confessional prayer that appears at the beginning of the EUCHARIST. Where confession is heard before a priest (confessor) in confidence and various PENANCES are given for ATONEMENT, the rite is considered to be one of the seven SACRAMENTS. Confession is also used to describe an official statement of faith concerned with doctrinal correctness. For example, during the REFORMATION, an emphasis was placed on 'confessions' meaning declarations of denominational loyalty through allegiance to statements of beliefs. (*See also* REDEMPTION; ROSARY)

Confessor   *See* CONFESSION.

Confirmation   The rite of passage and one of the seven SACRAMENTS which gives full entry into the Christian community and allows the person to share in the Communion. It usually takes the form of the laying on of hands, which is performed by a BISHOP, close to the onset of puberty. Confirmation completes the process begun at BAPTISM. The justifications for the rite come from a NEW TESTAMENT source that indicates that bishops were required to baptize in the HOLY SPIRIT after the initial water baptism carried out by DEACONS. However, the rite is first mentioned in 450 and may have come about as infant baptisms increased, in order to provide a strengthening of Christian commitment in new adulthood.

Congregationalism   A form of PURITAN Protestant dissent originating from the beliefs of Robert Browne (1550–1633) which developed from the idea that each local church should have autonomy and independence as practised in the early Church. The Congregationalist movement was influential in the English Civil War and was prominent in the army of Oliver Cromwell. The 1662 Act of Uniformity forced them to declare their position as NON-CONFORMISTS and resulted in their final break from the CHURCH OF ENGLAND. In 1972, the majority of the Congregationalists joined with the English PRESBYTERIANS to form the UNITED REFORMED CHURCH.

Congruism   The DOCTRINE that GRACE is given by God according to the performance of good works and to the circumstances in which it will be put to use. (*See also* JUSTIFICATION)

Consecration   The term used to describe either the ritual which sanctifies churches and ALTARS or the rite in which the bread and wine literally become or are associated with the body and blood of Christ. It takes place during the EUCHARIST after the offering of the elements to the altar and before the congregation participates in the Communion. The culmination of this consecration is the lifting up of the elements by the PRIEST in view of the entire congregation, and the solemn ringing of the sanctus bell. (*See also* HOST)

Constantine   (274–337). The Roman emperor who made Christianity the faith of the Empire by giving his imperial favour to the religion after winning the Battle of Milvian Bridge. He united the church and the state and in 325 summoned the various BISHOPS to the Council of NICAEA to resolve the issue of Arian CHRISTOLOGY and other disputes between Christians. In 330, he moved the capital of his Empire from Rome to Constantinople, which became the new capital of Eastern Christianity. (*See also* ARIANISM)

Consubstantiation   The belief that after CONSECRATION, the substances of the bread and wine and the body and blood of Christ exist in union with each other. Consubstantiation is particularly associated with Martin LUTHER and the Protestant traditions. Luther believed that both the bread and wine and the body of Christ are present in the EUCHARIST but there is no change of substance. The important point is to believe that Christ is present at the Eucharist. (*See also* TRANSUBSTANTIATION)

Convent   Although historically referring to a dwelling of a religious monastic community or the community itself, contemporary usage only applies to a community of NUNS or the building in which they reside. (*See also* MONK; ORDER; RELIGIOUS)

Cope   A semi-circular cloak worn by PRIESTS at the EUCHARIST. Its use in the CHURCH OF ENGLAND was revived in the nineteenth century under the influence of the OXFORD MOVEMENT. (*See also* VESTMENTS)

Corinthians, Epistles to the   Two NEW TESTAMENT EPISTLES written by PAUL to the Christian community at Corinth around 51–55. These are part of the undisputed letters whose authorship is attributed to Paul. The APOSTLE himself had helped to establish the church in Corinth and maintained close links with it. The letters were written to help the church deal with errors of belief arising from the influence of GNOSTICISM, misunderstandings of Paul's own teaching and perhaps to bring the church up to date with changes taking place in Paul's own thinking. The church had split into factions under several leaders and some Christians had written to Paul asking him to resolve various questions. The letters to the Corinthians are his response to all of the above factors.

Council   An assembly of BISHOPS and church leaders brought together from all over the Christian world in order to maintain discipline and unity by settling disputes over DOCTRINE or to effect major changes in church organization or LITURGY. Notable examples are the Councils of NICAEA in 325 and the VATICAN COUNCIL II from 1962 to 1965. (*See also* VATICAN COUNCIL I)

Credence A small side table placed near the ALTAR to hold the elements or the bread, wine and water that have been CONSECRATED and used at the EUCHARIST.

Creed A formal statement of religious belief which can be used to maintain ORTHODOX DOCTRINE and is held in common by all Christian believers. The most important are the APOSTLES' CREED and the NICENE CREED.

Crib In a custom of the Western Church, a representation of the crib or manger in which the newly born Christ was laid is placed in a church on CHRISTMAS Eve. It depicts the child Christ surrounded by the holy family, shepherds and the three MAGI or wise men.

Crosier The staff shaped like a shepherd's crook carried by a BISHOP and sometimes an ABBOT or ABBESS of a monastic community. The shepherd's crook is symbolic of Christ's role as the Good Shepherd or custodian of the Christian community.

Crucifix A model of the cross which carries the form of the crucified Christ. They are often worn around the neck on a chain or appear on the end of a ROSARY. Most Roman Catholic churches will contain statues or models of the crucified Christ above the ALTAR in the SANCTUARY. The plain cross without the crucified Christ is preferred in Protestant churches so that the emphasis is on the resurrected Christ. (*See also* CRUCIFIXION)

Crucifixion A common Roman punishment whereby a criminal or slave was put to death by being nailed or bound to a cross. The crucifixion of Jesus Christ was witnessed by the writers of all four GOSPELS, but they do not supply the details of Jesus' physical suffering other than to indicate that he refused to accept any aid. They are more concerned with the cosmic and soteriological significance of the event. The word 'cross' came to exemplify the gospel message that Jesus Christ, the Son of God, had died for human salvation through the ATONEMENT of all human sin. The cross has become a universal symbol of Christianity, and Christian discipleship is often perceived as cross-bearing or walking in the footsteps of Christ. (*See also* CRUCIFIX; REDEMPTION; SOTERIOLOGY)

Crusades A series of holy wars that took place between 1095 and 1464 ostensibly to reclaim the Holy Land from the Muslims. Although there were a number of economic reasons for taking part in the Crusades, and many probably took part for the material rewards of plunder and land and the spiritual rewards of forgiveness of sins, there were also religious reasons for the pious. The Crusader's life was perceived as an imitation of monastic life and a way of embarking on the road to spiritual perfection.

Curate A member of the clergy appointed to assist the parish PRIEST in the performance of his/her duties.

Curia The papal court which administers the Roman Catholic Church from the VATICAN. The term is also used for the officials of the CHAPTER who assist a diocesan BISHOP. (*See also* DIOCESE)

D

Damnation   The Christian belief in the possibility of punishment for SIN by passing an eternity in HELL. In the latter half of the twentieth century there were several theological challenges to the belief in a literal location for the damned soul. Others have questioned how a God of love could damn souls for ever based on sins committed in a short human lifespan. Many now perceive damnation as a state of alienation from the presence of God rather than an eternity in Hell. (*See also* PURGATORY; SATAN)

David (*c.* 970 BCE).   The first king of the Judaean dynasty and the second king of Israel. He is important in Christianity as it is affirmed in the NEW TESTAMENT that Jesus was born of the lineage of David. He is perceived as a foreshadower of Jesus Christ who is sometimes called 'the son of David'. Jesus himself is attributed with the words, 'I am the root and the offspring of David' (Revelation 22.16). This is important, as OLD TESTAMENT prophecies state that the MESSIAH would be a descendant of David. The PSALMS, which are used extensively in Christian LITURGY, are also traditionally attributed to David.

Deacon   From the Greek word *diakonia* (a servant or waiter at tables), the NEW TESTAMENT usually associates the function with pastoral or preaching activities. In the early Church, the function became more specialized as deacons were appointed to serve the poor and take care of the distribution of alms (Acts 6.1–6). They came below the BISHOP and the PRIEST in the episcopal hierarchy and exercised an administrative and social responsibility. In most Western episcopal churches the term is now used for the stage of preparation for priesthood and until recently defined the limit of female participation in the clergy. In the Eastern Church and many Protestant DENOMINATIONS, deacons function to care for the poor and the sick or administer alms. (*See also* DEACONESS)

Deaconess   The duties of a DEACON carried out by a woman probably goes back to the NEW TESTAMENT period where Phoebe is identified as the *diakonos* of the church at Cenchreae. Certainly the episcopal churches have never denied women access to the deaconate in the way that they have with the priesthood.

Dead Sea Scrolls   A library of Hebrew and Aramaic scrolls discovered on the north-west shore of the Dead Sea at QUMRAN in 1947 that provide insight into the political, religious and social organization of Hebrew life in the century before and after the life of Jesus Christ. In particular, they give considerable information on a semi-ascetic Jewish religious community known as the ESSENES, from whom they are believed to have originated.

Dean   The title given to the PRIEST in the episcopal churches who manages and administers the affairs of a CATHEDRAL. (*See also* ARCHBISHOP; BISHOP)

Decalogue   The Ten Commandments given by God to Moses on Mount Sinai, accepted by Christians as well as Jews. However, generally the Christian understanding of the law given by Moses differs in that the relationship of acceptance is based not on obedience but on intuitional or inner understanding of the relationship of love that exists between God and humans and between humans. Some have argued (for example, William Blake) that Christians are not bound to obey Jewish law but should rely on their intuitional awareness of love, following in the footsteps of Jesus Christ, who overruled the law when occasion demanded mercy or compassion.

Deism   A movement that became increasingly popular in France and Germany after the seventeenth century. Although it did accept that

God was the creator, it rejected the idea that God is still involved in the creation. Some individuals also rejected the idea of divine rewards, punishments and providence. Deism was never widely accepted in England, but there was a system of natural religion developed by a few prominent philosophers in the eighteenth century that was known by the same name.

Denominations   The term used to describe Christian movements or churches which are accepted as ORTHODOX by the WORLD COUNCIL OF CHURCHES. Denominationalism represents a move away from the church/sect model which promoted the view that one movement contained the doctrinal truth and others were merely breakaway heresies. Christian denominations accept their differences and acknowledge their unity, striving towards an ecumenical relationship with each other. (*See also* ECUMENISM)

Devil   *See* SATAN.

Diaconican   The area to the south of the sanctuary in an Eastern ORTHODOX CHURCH which is under the domain of the DEACON and where the VESTMENTS, prayer-books and sacred vessels used in the LITURGY are kept. (*See also* VESTRY)

Diocese   The territorial unit of administration under the control of a BISHOP, usually divided into parishes. In the Eastern Church it describes the territory under the control of a PATRIARCH.

Dirge   The traditional name for the Office of the Dead. (*See also* UNCTION)

Disciples   The term used to describe all those associated with Jesus and who responded to his message, particularly those that accompanied him on his travels. It can also be used to refer to the twelve men who gave him exclusive loyalty. (*See also* APOSTLES)

Dissenters   Those who separate themselves from the communion of the established Church, in particular, the CHURCH OF ENGLAND. After the

Restoration of the monarchy in 1660, the Act of Uniformity was passed in 1662 which forbade the use of any other service than that authorized by the revised Prayer Book. Effectively this move barred PURITANS from the Church and they were forced out of the establishment and became known as Dissenters. (*See also* NON-CONFORMISTS)

Docetism An early form of CHRISTOLOGY declared to be HERESY which maintained that the humanity and suffering of Jesus Christ was apparent rather than real. Christ was perceived to be a divine being and not human. Some forms of Docetism even maintained that Christ escaped the CRUCIFIXION. The criticism of Docetism is based on the view that if Christ is not human, then he loses any point of contact with those he came to save. His exemplary role becomes insignificant if not performed by someone who is not fully human. (*See also* IMITATION OF CHRIST; NESTORIAN)

Doctrine A body of teaching used as a standard of ORTHODOXY. In the NEW TESTAMENT it refers to a body of teaching given to those who respond to the call of the DISCIPLES to become followers of Christ. Over the centuries correct Christian doctrine was established by a series of councils and used to define HERESY. (*See also* DOGMA)

Dogma A religious truth that is first established by divine revelation and laid down in Scripture and then defined or interpreted by the Church. (*See also* DOCTRINE; HERESY)

Dominic, St (1170–1221) Born Dominic de Guzman near Castile in Spain, he entered the Augustinian Order. In 1206, he visited Languedoc and was surprised to discover the strength of the CATHARS and the general feeling of contempt for the CISTERCIAN ORDER amongst the local populace. He believed that the solution was a reform of the monastic orders so that they emulated the Cathars' piety, asceticism and zeal in preaching. As a result he established the DOMINICAN Order after visiting Rome for the Fourth Lateran Council.

Dominicans An order of friars founded by St DOMINIC in the thirteenth century which was devoted to study and preaching. The order was created as a reaction to the heretical CATHARS and Waldensians by providing preachers of equal devotion and asceticism. The order grew rapidly and by the fourteenth century contained over 600 houses throughout Europe, including several nunneries. The nuns of the order were enclosed and were renowned for their lives of poor humility. Their emphasis on study created an environment of learning and service in addition to evangelizing. The Dominicans were asked by Gregory IX in 1232 to form and staff the INQUISITION.

Dove   A well-known Christian symbol which denotes peace and reconciliation, the Church and the soul that has been saved through the rite of BAPTISM. It is also used to represent the HOLY SPIRIT. The symbol primarily derives from the incident of Jesus Christ's BAPTISM by JOHN THE BAPTIST when a dove appeared over Jesus' head as a manifestation of the Holy Spirit. It may also refer to the dove that appeared on the receding waters and made Noah aware that the survivors of the human race were reconciled to God.

E

Easter   The oldest and most important festival celebrating the RESUR-RECTION of Jesus Christ from the dead. The dates of Easter usually fall between the third week of March and the fourth week of April, depending on the date of the full moon. However, Eastern ORTHODOX CHURCHES do not observe Easter until the Jewish Passover is completed. Traditionally, Easter was a time which the early Church set aside for the BAPTISM of initiates. The holiday is preceded by the 40 days of traditional abstinence known as LENT, culminating in MAUNDY THURSDAY, which remembers the LAST SUPPER of Christ and his disciples before the vigil in the Garden of GETHSEMANE. GOOD FRIDAY commemorates the CRUCIFIXION. The festival culminates with the triumphant celebration of Easter Sunday when the RESURRECTION is remembered.

Ebionites   An ascetic sect of Jewish Christians from the early years of the development of Christianity. They emphasized the importance of the Mosaic law and played down the idea of the divinity of Jesus. It has come to be associated with any kind of heretical position in which Jesus Christ is treated merely as an enlightened human being and thus essentially the same as those who he came to redeem. (*See also* DOCETICM; HERESY)

Ecclesiology   An aspect of theology that deals with the theory or doctrine of the Church and attempts to provide justification for the institutional developments that have taken place throughout its history, often as a result of social and political change. (*See also* COUNCIL)

Ecumenism   The movement within the Church to reconcile and promote understanding between the DENOMINATIONS in the hope of restoring unity. Although the drive towards ecumenism has been notable in the twentieth-century development of Christianity, it has its roots in various historical developments extending as far back as the sixteenth century. Various factors, such as cooperation in missionary work, youth work, education, liturgical developments, common ethical actions and attempts to deal with doctrinal differences, have all contributed to the development of ecumenism. One of the great momentums for the ecumenical drive was the creation of the WORLD COUNCIL OF CHURCHES in 1948.

Eden   The original home of the first human beings, ADAM and EVE, before their fall into SIN and consequent expulsion. It is therefore a powerful symbol of the return of human beings to a state of GRACE brought about by the 'second Adam', a title given to Jesus in the NEW TESTAMENT. (*See also* ORIGINAL SIN)

Elders   A title given to officers in the PRESBYTERIAN churches. They are either teaching elders, whose duties are pastoral, or ruling elders, who are responsible under the pastor for administration. The term is probably derived from the OLD TESTAMENT where it is written in the Book of Exodus that the tribes of Israel were led by 70 elders possessed by the Spirit of God who assisted Moses in the governance of the people.

Election   The theological term describing an act of the divine will which chooses to save some of humankind from the moment of creation, whilst condemning others to eternal damnation. It is particularly associated with CALVINISM and PREDESTINATION. However, the OLD TESTAMENT is important in that it maintains that the Jewish tribes are the elect of God and chosen recipients of His covenant. The NEW TESTAMENT proclaims the extension of this covenant of salvation to the GENTILE world. It replaces the elect of the people of Israel with an elect who become the true Israel through faith in Jesus Christ.

Elevation The lifting of the bread and wine by the PRIEST after CONSE-CRATION in the Eucharistic rite introduced in 1200 in the Western Church. It is followed by the words 'Behold the Lamb of God who taketh away the sins of the world' and the ringing of the sanctus bells. In some churches, particularly Roman Catholic, the incense is directed towards the elevated HOST. (*See also* CHALICE; EUCHARIST)

Encyclical A circular letter sent out by the POPE to all the churches in order to provide new direction or DOCTRINE. (*See also* INFALLIBILITY)

Enthronization The ceremony in which an ARCHBISHOP or a BISHOP is placed in possession of his throne in a CATHEDRAL and appointed with ecclesiastical authority over a DIOCESE.

Ephesians, Epistle to the One of the books of the NEW TESTAMENT, apparently written to the early church in Ephesus by St PAUL when he was in prison. This has been questioned by some scholars on the grounds that both the language and the content differ from other letters written by Paul. The letter makes no attempt to address contro-versies or to involve itself in pastoral concerns of the early Christian communities. Instead, it focuses on the eternal purposes of God and the manifestion of Christ in the church. (*See also* EPISTLES)

Epiphany The twelfth and final day of CHRISTMAS in the Christian litur-gical year and maintained on 6 January. Traditionally, it celebrates the MAGI's bestowing of gifts on the new born Christ. This is considered to be a symbol of the acknowledgement of Christ by the GENTILES as the Magi were the first non-Jews to recognize and venerate Christ. The Epiphany is also associated with Christ's BAPTISM and the first miracle in Cana, when Jesus turned water into wine at a wedding feast.

Episcopacy A system of church government by BISHOPS, who maintain a hierarchy of bishops, PRIESTS and laity most familiarly associated with Roman Catholicism. The authority for the Episcopalian leadership rests in the APOSTOLIC SUCCESSION, which asserts an unbroken line of male priestly authority from the original APOSTLES through the leaders of the early Church to the bishops of today. Although Episcopalian authority was challenged at the Protestant REFORMATION, it is still maintained by some Protestant groups known as the Episcopal churches. They include the ANGLICAN COMMUNION and METHODISM. (*See also* CHURCH OF ENGLAND)

Epistle   *Lit. letter*. Several letters circulated from the first leaders of the Christian community to the various churches that were beginning to spring up around the Mediterranean Greek world and included in the NEW TESTAMENT. There are 21 in total, of which most are attributed to PAUL, and include letters to the ROMANS, COLOSSIANS, EPHESIANS, PHILIPPIANS, CORINTHIANS, GALATIANS and THESSALONIANS, along with the personal letters to TIMOTHY and TITUS and PHILEMON. The remaining epistles are attributed to JOHN, JUDE, JAMES and PETER. (*See also* JAMES, EPISTLE OF; JOHN, EPISTLES OF; PETER, EPISTLES OF)

Essenes   The Jewish ascetic community most commonly associated with the DEAD SEA SCROLLS. They probably existed from the second century BCE to the second century CE. They established a community at QUMRAN where the Dead Sea Scrolls were discovered. They were highly organized and communalistic. Some scholars have suggested that JOHN THE BAPTIST was a former member of the community and there has been considerable speculation about the influence of the Essenes on the teachings of Jesus.

Eternal life   The term used in the GOSPEL of St. JOHN to describe the special quality of life enjoyed by the followers of Jesus Christ. Although often used by Christians to refer to an eternal duration in Paradise after death, it can also refer to the possession of the here and now through joining with God's eternal being. (*See also* HEAVEN; REDEMPTION)

Eucharist   *Lit. thanksgiving*. One of the several terms, including Lord's Supper, MASS and Holy Communion, used to name the central act of worship in the Christian tradition. It is derived from the LAST SUPPER or Passover meal which Jesus Christ celebrated with his disciples. On that occasion, immediately prior to his death, he broke bread and drank wine with the disciples and asked them to follow the practice in remembrance of him. The Eucharist, therefore, celebrates the sacrificial death and RESURRECTION of Jesus Christ by using the elements of bread and wine as an offering. The Christian Church is divided over the significance of what takes place at the Eucharist. The basic division is between those who believe that the elements are changed into the substance of the body of Christ and those who prefer to make the lesser claim that they are powerful symbols or reminders of the origins of the Christian faith. (*See also* CONSUBSTANTIATION; TRANSUBSTANTIATION)

Evangelical   A group or church which places particular emphasis on the Scriptures as the only authority in matters of faith and conduct. It was first used in the sixteenth century to refer to Catholic writers who wished to place more emphasis on the authority of Scripture than medieval church tradition, but is now used to describe any group of Christians across the DENOMINATIONS who place particular emphasis on the BIBLE in Christian life. Most EVANGELISTS subscribe to four assumptions concerning the reality of being a Christian, which include the fundamental tenet of following the authority of Scripture. The other three are the uniqueness of REDEMPTION through the CRUCIFIXION and RESURRECTION of Jesus Christ, the need for a personal redemptive experience and the urgent necessity of preaching the GOSPEL. (*See also* CHARISMATIC; FUNDAMENTALISM)

Evangelist   Used in the NEW TESTAMENT to denote someone who 'announces news' and usually rendered in translation as 'preach the gospel'. Scripture utilizes the term for the work of God, Jesus Christ, the APOSTLES and even ordinary members of the fledgling Church. It is now used for anyone who commits his or her life to spreading the Christian message. More specifically it is used to describe the writers of the four GOSPELS. (*See also* EVANGELICAL)

Eve   The first woman and partner of ADAM. The ORIGINAL SIN and FALL of humankind from the GRACE of God is attributed to Eve giving in to the temptation of SATAN and eating the forbidden fruit of the tree of knowledge. (*See also* EDEN)

Evensong   The common name given to the CHURCH OF ENGLAND and ANGLICAN evening prayer service which has conflated the two divine OFFICES of VESPERS and COMPLINE. It consists of PSALMS, a lesson from the OLD TESTAMENT, the MAGNIFICAT, a LESSON from the NEW TESTAMENT, the NUNC DIMITTIS, the APOSTLES' CREED and some prayers.

Excommunication   The term used to describe exclusion from the communion of the faithful of any member who, perceived to have committed a serious offence, has failed to be corrected by educative means or the application of church discipline. The gradual progression to the final exclusion consists of private and then witnessed remonstrance. If this repeatedly fails, the offender should be dealt with by officials of the church. Excommunication is primarily intended to invoke REPENTANCE but it is also designed to protect other church members from contamination. In the Roman Catholic church, while it denies the possibility of administering or receiving the SACRAMENTS, the offender may still attend the preaching of the Word. Although it is now rarely applied, historically it has generally been used to control doctrinal HERESY.

Expiation   A theological term generally applied to the sacrifice of Jesus Christ on the Cross, by which act he made amends for the inherited SIN of mankind which began with the FALL of ADAM and EVE. (*See also* CRUCIFIXION; RANSOM; REDEMPTION)

Faith   In Christianity faith means more than a commitment to belief without any empirical evidence. It is, first of all, a body of truth as propounded in DOCTRINE which accepts as true the articles of the faith as summarized in the CREEDS. However, it was Martin LUTHER who made the point that faith is fundamental to Christian salvation. He asserted that faith is the human response to the truth-claim of Christian doctrine and is the right relationship to have with God. Lost at the FALL and resurrected by the INCARNATION of Jesus Christ, it is, therefore, regarded as a supernatural act of will and a higher faculty than reason.

Fall, the   The first act of disobedience to God committed by ADAM and EVE in the Garden of EDEN. In the well-known story from Genesis, Eve persuaded Adam to eat the fruit of the 'tree of knowledge of good and evil' and thus both lost their primal innocence. As punishment they were expelled from the Garden of Eden. The consequences were that all human beings were henceforth in a fallen state – that is, subject to SIN and born to a lesser condition than God had originally prepared for them. Christ's birth, life and death atoned for this act of ORIGINAL SIN and provided the means for recovery from the fallen condition. (*See also* ATONEMENT; GRACE; RESURRECTION)

Feretory   A shrine where a SAINT's bones are kept and venerated. (*See also* RELICS; RELIQUARY)

Filioque   The addition of the words '*and from the son*' to the sentence which states that the Holy Ghost '*proceedeth from the Father*' contained in the NICENE CREED and normative in the Western Church. The Eastern Church disagreed and argued that both the Son and the HOLY SPIRIT proceed from the Father. They argued that the Father must be not be compromised as the sole source of divinity. It was, therefore, one of the principal causes of doctrinal dispute between the Eastern and Western churches and contributed to the division between them.

Fish   A symbol for Christ used in Christian iconography which originated in the time of the early Church from the fact that the letters of the Greek word *ichthys* (fish) were also the initials of *Iesous Christos Theou Hyios Soter* (Jesus Christ, of God the Son, Saviour). The NEW TESTAMENT contains many references to fish, arising from the exploits of Jesus around GALILEE and from the fact that several of his first followers were fishermen.

Font   Receptacle, usually made of stone, which stands at the west end of the NAVE and holds the water used for the sacrament of BAPTISM. The ceremony at the font consists of procession, renunciation of SATAN, profession of FAITH, immersion in water, and sometimes anointing with oil.

Form Criticism   A method of analysis which attempts to discover the origin of particular passages in the Old and New Testaments through exploring the variety of structural forms. The aim is to ascertain the earliest forms of the texts, possibly in the oral tradition, and then to establish the historical context in which they developed into later written forms.

Formal Sin   *See* SIN.

Forty-two Articles   The statements of correct ANGLICAN DOCTRINE devised in 1553 by Archbishop Cranmer and signed by Edward VI. Although Protestant in tone, they were designed to offset ANABAPTIST doctrines as well as Roman Catholicism. Their number was revised to 39 in 1563 during the reign of Elizabeth I. (*See also* THIRTY-NINE ARTICLES).

Fraction   The ritual breaking of bread by the PRIEST which takes place in all Eucharistic LITURGIES before the act of Communion. (*See also* CONSECRATION; EUCHARIST; OFFERTORY)

Francis of Assisi, St   (1181–1226) Born Giovanni Bernardone in the central Italian city of Assisi, he was the founder of the FRANCISCAN ORDER. Although he was worldly as a young man, he gradually turned to religion as a result of experiences arising from illness and participating in warfare. He began to rebuild churches in the area of Assisi after a vision in which God commanded him to 'rebuild my Church'. In 1208, aware that he had received the same call as the APOSTLES, he began to preach REPENTANCE. Francis lived in complete poverty and modelled his lifestyle on that of Christ. He remains one of the most loved saints in Christianity because of his humility, devotion to God, love of nature and compassion.

Franciscans   The ORDER of FRIARS founded by St FRANCIS OF ASSISI in 1210 and licensed to preach by Pope Innocent III. Renouncing worldly pleasures and living a life of absolute poverty, they preach the GOSPEL and take care of the needy and the sick. The organization of the order is similar to that of the DOMINICANS and they also have a female order known as the POOR CLARES. The growth of the order was rapid, especially in the cities, where they were successful in strengthening religion amongst the laity. The Franciscans have a tertiary order open to pious individuals who are allowed to live a semi-monastic life of fasting, prayer and good deeds.

Free Churches   NON-CONFORMIST Protestant denominations which are free from state control.

Friar   A member of one of the mendicant ORDERS founded in the Middle Ages. They were not allowed to maintain or own property and moved around begging or working for their living. They were exempt from the control of the diocesan BISHOP and passed their time in preaching and receiving confession. (*See also* FRANCISCANS)

Friends, Society of   *See* QUAKERS.

Fundamentalism   American EVANGELICAL movements which arose in opposition to secularization in the second half of the twentieth century. Fundamentalism is characterized by its literal interpretation of Scripture and its animosity to any form of Biblical criticism. It asserts the imminent return of Christ before the end of time.

G

Gabriel   *Lit. man of god or strength of God.* One of the four ARCHANGELS with special responsibility over HEAVEN and a functionary of the LAST JUDGEMENT. In the NEW TESTAMENT, Gabriel is sent to announce the birth of JOHN THE BAPTIST to his father, ZACHARIAH and to announce the conception of Jesus Christ to MARY.

Galatians, Epistle to the   One of the earliest of the books in the NEW TESTAMENT. It was written by PAUL, somewhere between 49 and 53 CE, to the Christian community in Galatia in order to clarify the relationship between FAITH in Christ and obedience to the Jewish law. Paul affirms his authority as coming directly from Christ and warns against the dangers of mixing the Christian message of salvation for all with Jewish legalism. (*See also* EPISTLES)

Galilee   The district between the coastal strip of the Mediterranean and the River JORDAN in the north of Israel which contains the town of NAZARETH, where Jesus grew to adulthood. Jesus spent most of his life and ministry in Galilee and the first DISCIPLES came from the region. The Sea of Galilee is a local lake, also known as Gennesaret or the Sea of Tiberias. The shores of the lake contain the towns of Bethsaida and CAPERNAUM, where much of Christ's ministry took place.

General   The head of a religious order. For example, the head of the FRANCISCANS is known as the Minister-General, while the head of the DOMINICANS is called the Master-General. (*See also* BENEDICTINES; JESUITS)

Geneva Bible   The English Bible published in Geneva in 1560 by the Protestant exiles from the reign of the Catholic queen Mary Tudor and widely used for 50 years until the publication of the AUTHORIZED VERSION in 1611.

Gentiles   The term used in the NEW TESTAMENT to describe non-Jews. Israelites had come to develop a sense of themselves as a distinct nation chosen by God after the revelation of the covenant to Moses. By the time of Jesus, an exclusive attitude to other nations had developed as a result of efforts to maintain Judaism's purity despite other cultural accretions. Jewish prophecies had always indicated that the expected MESSIAH would restore righteousness throughout the world. Therefore, the stage was set for the Jewish disciples of Jesus to consider the possibility that his message was also for non-Jews. The conversion of Cornelius and the mission of PAUL to bring the Gentiles to Christ's salvation initially created misgivings and soul-searching amongst the Jewish followers of Jesus, but the growing Church quickly adapted to the idea of equality of all people before God.

Genuflexion   A movement down on to one knee and then up to the standing position again. It is commonly used in the Western Church to show reverence when passing before the reserved SACRAMENT or on other ritual occasions.

Gethsemane   The garden just outside the walls of JERUSALEM near the Mount of Olives to the east of the city. The garden was frequently used by Jesus and his DISCIPLES as a place of retreat, and it is here that Jesus passed the night in prayer with his disciples before betrayal by JUDAS ISCARIOT and his arrest. The descriptions of Christ's vigil of prayer in St. Mark's Gospel have given rise to the practice of kneeling in prayer which is customary amongst Christians. (*See also* CRUCIFIXION; MAUNDY THURSDAY; PASSION)

Glossolalia   Known as 'speaking in tongues', it describes a religious phenomenon where the person is possessed by the HOLY SPIRIT and speaks in an unknown language. It was first recorded in the NEW TESTAMENT (Acts 2.4) when the APOSTLES preached on the feast of

PENTECOST and were understood by people as speaking many different languages. Contemporary manifestations of glossolalia include the utterance in an unknown tongue rather than the ability to speak and be understood in several languages. The gift of glossolalia also requires the gift of interpretation in order for the congregation to comprehend the words of the Spirit. This may be a result of PAUL's criticism that it was more important to preach the GOSPEL than to speak in unknown languages (Corinthians 14.19). However, Paul did not denigrate glossolalia and it is considered to be a gift from the Holy Spirit, featuring in several Christian revival movements, particularly the PENTECOSTALIST movement.

Gnosticism   Derived from the Greek word *gnosis* meaning knowledge, it is an umbrella term to describe a host of movements, both Christian and non-Christian, who believed in a special knowledge of God which leads to enlightenment or REDEMPTION. Some of the movements were very strong at the time of the early Church but were opposed because they minimized the role of FAITH in salvation and maintained heretical positions in regard to the status of Christ. The common feature of all the Gnostic movements was a dualistic cosmology based on the belief that the created world was evil and completely separate from the perfect world of the spirit. Matter was not created by God but by a lesser spirit known as the demiurge. Gnosis, or knowledge, allows the recipient to liberate the soul from the bondage of matter, usually through the intervention of a redeemer who descends from the spiritual world. The Gnostic quest is therefore redemption through discovery of the soul as one's real identity. The early church fathers fought against Gnostic influences in Christianity and regarded it as a perversion of Christ's teaching.

Good Friday   The Friday of HOLY WEEK, which precedes EASTER Sunday, it commemorates the CRUCIFIXION of Jesus Christ. Normally the LITURGY of Good Friday does not feature the celebration of the EUCHARIST, but in Roman Catholicism there is a service known as the Veneration of the Cross that developed in the third and fourth centuries, in which the CLERGY and the congregation solemnly venerate a cross close to the SANCTUARY area. Good Friday is normally a time of fasting, PENANCE and ABSTINENCE.

Gospel   *Lit. the good news.* The message of salvation through Jesus Christ proclaimed through Christian mission especially in the apostolic period. The term came to be used for the written accounts of Jesus Christ that form the first four books of the NEW TESTAMENT. The Gospels contain Jesus' message that the time appointed for the kingdom of God had arrived as a fulfilment of the prophecies communicated through the Jewish prophets. This message is reinforced by parables and examples of teaching sessions with the DISCIPLES and confrontation with Jewish religious leaders. The gospels also contain Jesus' actions, including accounts of his miracles. However, the dominant emphasis is on the events leading to the CRUCIFIXION and RESURRECTION. The Gospels can be dated to somewhere between 60 and 100, and although there has been some debate concerning their authorship, it is generally acknowledged that St John's Gospel is uniquely different to the other three SYNOPTIC GOSPELS (*See also* JOHN, GOSPEL OF; LUKE, GOSPEL OF; MARK, GOSPEL OF; MATTHEW, GOSPEL OF).

Grace   The freely given and unmerited favour of God's love, which breaks the hold of SIN on the human being. Christian DOCTRINE asserts that human beings do not have the essential qualities required for their own salvation, as the human will was corrupted by sin. Humans can never enter into a relationship with God as a result of their own efforts; the process of salvation can only be initiated by God through the birth, death and RESURRECTION of Jesus Christ. Grace is also a term for a prayer of thanksgiving normally made before a meal.

Habit The distinctive outer garb of a male or female member of a religious order. (*See also* FRIAR; MONK; NUN)

Halo A circle of light that appears around the head of Jesus Christ, the Virgin MARY and the SAINTS in traditional Christian iconography, to represent the presence of God or divinity.

Harvest Thanksgiving An unofficial festival of thanksgiving for the produce of the earth celebrated in Britain usually in September or October. The festival is marked by the bringing of produce to the church and replaces the older pagan Harvest Home festivals.

Heaven The dwelling place of God and the ANGELS, also known as paradise, and the place or state of being in which redeemed souls or SAINTS will be united with God after death. Heaven is also used in an eschatological sense to indicate the final and perfect condition of creation after the second coming of Christ, when all things will fully express the will of God. This is expressed in the line of the LORD'S PRAYER which states 'Thy Kingdom come on Earth as it is in Heaven'. (*See also* PAROUSIA)

Hebrews, Epistle to the One of the books of the NEW TESTAMENT attributed to PAUL, although very few modern scholars would acknowledge Pauline authorship. The EPISTLE was probably written to Jewish Christians to warn them of the dangers of returning to Judaism, or it may have been an attempt to convince Jewish

Christians of the new universal context to the faith. The author addresses the issue of the new covenant of God given through Jesus Christ which replaces the old covenant given to the people of Israel.

Hell The place or state of being for unredeemed souls after death, reserved for unrepentant sinners and the consequence of removal from the presence of God. The NEW TESTAMENT is unequivocal regarding hell and states that its fires are unquenchable and eternal. Jesus Christ warns of the undoubted reality of God's punishment for evil-doers in the afterlife. There has been debate as to whether a merciful and loving God could consign all sinners to eternal punishment with no hope of salvation. In recent times this debate has extended to incorporate the idea that hell is a state of being rather than a location. (*See also* PURGATORY)

Heresy *Lit. choice*. The denial of ORTHODOX DOCTRINE or the belief in a doctrine which has been officially declared unorthodox and heretical. The word refers to anyone who chooses to follow their own way or to form their own group. Although the NEW TESTAMENT use of heresy to mean doctrinal error only occurs in one of the letters of Peter, that became the general meaning throughout the history of Christianity. Major schisms have resulted over interpretations of Christ's identity and often Christian COUNCILS were called to resolve doctrinal divisions by asserting orthodoxy and declaring divergent opinions as heresy. Once Christianity became a state religion, heresy was likely to be punished as a crime. (*See also* ARIANISM; CHRISTOLOGY, EBIONITES; INQUISITION)

High Altar The main ALTAR of a church that traditionally stands at the entrance to the SANCTUARY at the east end of the NAVE.

High Church The group within the CHURCH OF ENGLAND which emphasizes its continuity with Catholic Christianity and places the same emphasis on the seven SACRAMENTS and the importance of the episcopate as Roman Catholicism. This wing of the Church of England, also known as Anglo-Catholic, has existed since the Tudor period but declined during the seventeenth and eighteenth centuries.

It was revived under the influence of the OXFORD MOVEMENT in the nineteenth century. (*See also* TRACTARIANISM)

Holy Communion   *See* EUCHARIST.

Holy Ghost   *See* HOLY SPIRIT.

Holy Orders   The membership of the priesthood either as BISHOP, PRIEST or DEACON.

Holy See   The spiritual and temporal domain of the POPE (*See also* ROMAN CATHOLIC; SEE; VATICAN).

Holy Sepulchre   The church in JERUSALEM, which is built over the cave where Jesus Christ is believed to have been buried after the CRUCI-FIXION and prior to his RESURRECTION. The first church on the site was built in 335. The present church contains several CHAPELS which represent the main strands of Christianity that maintain a historical presence in Jerusalem. (*See also* CALVARY)

Holy Spirit / Holy Ghost   The third person of the Holy TRINITY, sometimes referred to as the Comforter, is the Spirit of God. The OLD TESTAMENT utilizes images of wind and breath (*ruach*) to indicate the life-giving and refreshing properties of God's presence in creation. However, both the Old and NEW TESTAMENT refer to the function of the Spirit in filling an individual with God's presence, which then acts as a guide, inspiration or motivator and possibly the provider of divine gifts such as healing or prophecy. It is believed that after the ASCENSION of Christ, the Holy Spirit continued the redemptive work of God in the world and came down upon the APOSTLES at the Feast of PENTECOST. It is therefore active as God's presence in the world and some Christian groups, such as PENTECOSTALISTS and CHARISMATICS place emphasis on this aspect of divinity. (*See also* GLOSSOLALIA)

Holy Water   Water that has been blessed for religious purposes and used for blessings, exorcisms and ritual purification of a church. It is not to be confused with the water used for BAPTISM.

Holy Week   The week which culminates in EASTER Sunday and is observed by Christians in remembrance of Christ's last week on Earth.

Homoiousios   *Lit. of one substance.* The term used in the NICENE CREED to indicate the ORTHODOX CHRISTOLOGICAL relationship between the Father and the Son which asserts that Jesus Christ was of the same substance as God. The DOCTRINE was in opposition to the ARIAN heresy that Christ was a similar substance. (*See also* NICAEA, COUNCIL OF; TRINITARIAN; TRINITY)

Hope   One of the three theological virtues along with FAITH and LOVE as taught by PAUL. Paul uses hope in a special sense, describing pagans or non-Christians as a people without hope, as they were without God. In its widest sense, it can be used to celebrate the possibility of finding the highest good that is one's ultimate end in God, but in Christian terms it also refers to the faith in a living God who intervenes in human history and individuals' lives to fulfil His promises of salvation. Paul links hope with faith and love, and states that they are the fundamental features of Christian life.

Hosanna   A celebratory word employed in Christian LITURGY that was first used by the crowds that celebrated Jesus' triumphal entry into JERUSALEM on PALM SUNDAY. It is difficult to ascertain whether this was spontaneous or a traditional greeting with palms that originated in the Jewish feast of Sukkot.

Hospitallers   The Knights of St John, who were founded in JERUSALEM by Raymond du Poys (1120–60), the grand master of the hospital named after JOHN THE BAPTIST. He turned the foundation into a military order similar to that of the TEMPLARS, although it was committed to maintaining its medical work. The order successfully resisted the Turks and Moors from the Mediterranean islands of Rhodes and Malta. (*See also* CRUSADES)

Host   The CONSECRATED bread considered to be the sacrificed body of Christ. (*See also* EUCHARIST; TRANSUBSTANTIATION)

Huguenots   The name given to CALVINIST French Protestants who, in their desire to convert, caused France to be divided by a series of religious wars between the Catholic majority and the Protestant minority in the sixteenth century. Following their decline after the massacre of St Bartholomew's Day and a period of persecution during the sixteenth century, they finally won the right to freedom of worship in 1593.

Humanae Vitae   The ENCYCLICAL of the POPE in 1968 which affirmed the traditional opposition of the Roman Catholic Church to abortion and all contraception except for the rhythm method. It came after the more liberalizing influence of the changes brought about in VATICAN COUNCIL II and in spite of a special commission that had advocated a change in position. As a result, thousands left the priesthood and religious orders.

Humility   Humility is perceived as being an aspect of God's nature, in that being all-powerful he still partakes in creation. The greatest act of humility in Christianity is God incarnating as Jesus Christ and suffering CRUCIFIXION. PAUL suggests that humility was practised by Jesus Christ and culminated in his eventual victory over death and ASCENSION to the right hand of God. There is a sense throughout the both the OLD and NEW TESTAMENTS that tribulations or trials are sent to provide the opportunity to develop humility. As a virtue it is considered essential for progress in spiritual life, and Paul warns Christians to look out for those who put on false humility. (*See also* SEVEN VIRTUES)

Hymns   The Greek word *hymnos* is used for any song that praises a god or hero, but in Christianity it has come to denote religious poetry set to music that forms a key part of communal worship. However, the practice is an ancient one and the NEW TESTAMENT records examples of the first Christians singing as an expression of spontaneous joy in their experience of salvation. (*See also* PSALMS)

I

Ichthus   *Lit. fish.* The letters of the Greek word for 'fish' form the initials of 'Jesus Christ, Son of God, Saviour'. In the early Church, the FISH was used as a symbol of Christianity, sometimes even as a secret communication of belonging for Christians who were being persecuted.

Icon   One-dimensional paintings and mosaics of Jesus Christ, MARY or the Christian SAINTS used in the Eastern ORTHODOX CHURCHES as an aid for devotion or a window to the divine. Believed to contain the presence of the divine, they are used at all the important events of human life or rites of passage. (*See also* ICONOSTASIS)

Iconostasis   A screen covered in icons and containing two doors used to separate the ALTAR from the NAVE in Eastern churches. The screen functions to divide the PRIESTS from the laity during the LITURGY or celebration of Communion.

Imago Dei   *Lit. image of God.* The DOCTRINE that human beings are created in the image of God as recounted in Genesis. The early church fathers tended to interpret this as the potential of human beings, through reason and GRACE, to stand above the rest of creation in their relationship to God.

Imitation of Christ   The DOCTRINE that Jesus Christ was not only the means of salvation through his death and RESURRECTION but also the perfect exemplar of, or paradigm for, the redeemed life. The medieval writer and mystic Thomas à Kempis' work *Imitation of Christ* provides an example of the view that the Christian should look to Christ as the epitome of the ideal relationship between a human being and God.

Immaculate Conception The DOCTRINE that MARY, the mother of Jesus, was free from sin at her conception and remained so throughout her life. It was championed by Duns Scotus (1265–1308) and had become the dominant doctrine by the end of the Middle Ages. The position is still maintained by Roman Catholicism but was discarded by the Protestant reformers. (*See also* VIRGIN BIRTH)

Immersion A method of BAPTISM where the candidate is partially or completely immersed in water and in which water is poured over the head. Generally, this form of baptism takes place in Protestant DENOMINATIONS who insist upon adult baptism that resembles as closely as possible that employed by JOHN THE BAPTIST with Jesus. Eastern ORTHODOX traditions also immerse babies. (*See also* BAPTISTS; INFANT BAPTISM).

Impediment A legal or moral obstacle standing in the way of Christian marriage. Normally, the priest will ask the guests attending the wedding if they know of any just cause as to why the union of the man and woman cannot take place. (*See also* CANON LAW)

Incarnation The DOCTRINE that God became human in the form of Jesus Christ. Although the theological term 'incarnation' does not appear in the Bible, several of the NEW TESTAMENT writers indicate that the belief in Christ as the incarnate Son of God was already developed. For example, St PAUL argues that God sent His Son 'in the likeness of sinful flesh' (Romans 8.3). Although the New Testament is clear that the birth, life and death of Jesus were fully human events, in some way God never ceased to be God although fully manifested as a human being. Thus, Christian ORTHODOXY asserts that the historical Jesus is at once fully human and fully divine. (*See also* ATONEMENT; CHRISTOLOGY; LOGOS)

Incumbent The term used in the CHURCH OF ENGLAND for the member of the CLERGY in charge of a PARISH. (*See also* VICAR)

Indulgences / Pardon The authority of the Roman Catholic Church to provide remission of the temporal punishment for SINS either in this life or PURGATORY. There has been much controversy over the practice of selling indulgences and this was one of the causes of LUTHER's dissatisfaction with the Roman Catholic Church. While it is certainly the case that donations were originally given to good causes by grateful penitents, the system was open to abuse, allowing penitents to believe that they could buy indulgence from their sins and therefore avoid divine punishment. (*See also* ABSOLUTION; CONFESSION)

Infallibility The Roman Catholic DOCTRINE that in certain situations the Church or the POPE cannot make errors in teaching revealed truth. Since 1870, the Pope has been considered to be infallible when defining a doctrine on FAITH or morality. (*See also* VATICAN COUNCIL I)

Infant Baptism Although not clearly mentioned in the NEW TESTAMENT, there is also no condemnation of the practice. Since at least the third century, children of Christians have been baptized in infancy. However, although widespread there was opposition – for example, from Tertullian, who argued that the new Christian should be old enough to know Christ. Counter-arguments stated that REDEMPTION must be available for all, including children. It is also possible that it replaced the Jewish rite of circumcision as a rite of passage for young Christians. There is still controversy over infant baptism. The main arguments for the practice state that infant baptism remits the guilt of ORIGINAL SIN and provides affirmation of membership of the Christian community, which is built upon a covenant between God and His Church. The main argument against the practice was strengthened after the REFORMATION and consists of the viewpoint that BAPTISM should occur only after recognition has taken place that redemption is required through the GRACE and mercy of Jesus Christ. In the Eastern Church, infant baptism is followed by immediate communion but the Western Church follows the practice of providing CONFIRMATION in late childhood which allows for conscious full participation in the Christian community. (*See also* IMMERSION)

Inquisition A permanent institution established for the persecution of HERESY by specially convened ecclesiastical courts. It was introduced in 1232 by Pope Gregory IX and finally suppressed in 1820. The task of rooting out heresy and trying the heretics was entrusted to the DOMINICAN order who set up their own courts virtually independent from any local church authority, the proceedings of which were shrouded in secrecy. The heretics who recanted were given PENANCE to perform, while those who refused to admit their guilt were handed over to the secular authorities, where they were usually burned to death at the stake.

J

James, Epistle of   A book of the NEW TESTAMENT written as a letter to the churches concerning moral matters. Traditionally, its authorship, although disputed, is ascribed to JAMES, the brother of Jesus who was the leader of the early Church in JERUSALEM. With the emphasis on moral and ethical matters, the author seems to be asserting the DOCTRINE of JUSTIFICATION through works rather than the Pauline position of justification through faith. This has led to the epistle being used as part of the doctrinal struggle between Roman Catholicism and Protestantism. LUTHER, for example, devalued the writings, whereas Roman Catholicism has always used the contents to support justification by works, personal confession and the sacrament of unction. (*See also* EPISTLE)

James, St   The brother of Jesus Christ and the first leader of the Jewish Christian Church in JERUSALEM. It is generally believed that he did not accept Jesus' authority until receiving a vision of the risen Christ after the RESURRECTION. James presided over the Council of Jerusalem which debated with PAUL the issue of allowing GENTILES to become Christians. He worked to maintain unity with Paul and was finally martyred by stoning in 61 CE. (*See also* JAMES, ST (THE GREAT); JAMES, ST (THE LESS))

James, St (the Great)   One of the original twelve APOSTLES chosen by Jesus Christ as companions and missionaries. He was the elder brother of St JOHN and the son of Zebedee, a Galilean fisherman. The two brothers were nicknamed 'sons of thunder' by Jesus and, along with PETER, formed the privileged band allowed to witness the TRANS-FIGURATION and the agony of Jesus in the garden of GETHSEMANE. (*See also* JAMES, ST; JAMES, ST (THE LESS))

James, St (the Less) Also known as 'the younger'. One of the original twelve APOSTLES who were chosen by Jesus Christ as his companions and missionaries. He is known as 'the Less' to distinguish him from James, the brother of John. St Mark's Gospel indicates that he was the son of Alphaeus (*See also* JAMES, ST; JAMES, ST (THE GREAT)).

Jehovah's Witnesses A sect founded in the USA by Charles T. Russell (1852–1916), also known as the Watch Tower Bible and Tract Society. They are best known for their door-to-door ministry and their beliefs concerning the near end of the world and the millennium, when it was believed that only an ELECT chosen from amongst the witnesses would become members of the messianic kingdom established after the physical resurrection of the dead. (*See also* ADVENTIST)

Jerusalem The ancient and modern capital of Israel and the location of the final short period of Christ's ministry and his subsequent arrest, trial, CRUCIFIXION and RESURRECTION. It was also the place where the DISCIPLES lived and taught immediately after the death of Christ and it was the centre of the Jewish/Christian church under the leadership of JAMES, the brother of Jesus Christ. The city was visited by St Helena, the wife of the Roman emperor, CONSTANTINE, in 326. She is believed to have identified all the places associated with Jesus' life and death by miraculous means. Since that time the city has been a famous Christian centre of pilgrimage.

Jesuit The Society of Jesus founded by St Ignatius LOYOLA in 1534. Its intentions were to reform the Roman Catholic Church, in order to answer Protestant criticisms, and to engage in missionary work in the recently discovered parts of the world. Members of the order take a vow of absolute obedience to the POPE. The order is famous for its intellectualism and missionary endeavours. Ignatius himself established missions in India, Japan, China, Ethiopia, Malaysia and Brazil. Although suppressed in Latin Europe during the eighteenth century, they were restored in 1814. Members of the order do not wear a distinctive habit and are exempt from reciting the OFFICE communally.

Jesus Christ   The central figure of FAITH and devotion for all Christians, who was born shortly before the death of Herod the Great in 4 BCE and met his death by crucifixion somewhere close to 33 CE. Little is known about Jesus' life other than the accounts written in the four GOSPELS, which are generally concerned to present the Jesus of faith and focus on miracle stories, the events of his death and RESUR-RECTION and some teachings. The Gospels provide details of Jesus' birth and childhood, the beginning of his public ministry, including his baptism by JOHN THE BAPTIST, his temptation by SATAN whilst in retreat in the Judean desert, and his move to GALILEE and recruiting of his first DISCIPLES. They then describe his teachings, miracles and his disputes with the Jewish religious leaders over the issue of tradi-tional authority. Much of the Gospel narratives are concerned with the events leading up to the CRUCIFIXION in JERUSALEM. Whatever the historical reality of the life and death of Jesus, he is regarded by the early followers of his message to be the INCARNATION of God, and this DOCTRINE remains the bedrock upon which most Christian DENOMI-NATIONS found their faith. It is central to Christian belief that Jesus Christ was born as a divine sacrifice in order to provide the possibility of salvation to all human beings through his death and resurrection. He restores humanity from the fallen state induced by the ORIGINAL SIN of ADAM and EVE. (*See also* CHRISTOLOGY)

Jesus Movement   A collection of EVANGELICAL groups which emerged out of the alternative youth culture in the 1960s, especially in California. Sometimes known as 'Jesus People', they are known for their fervour, which combines spontaneity of worship and lifestyle with traditional morality and literalist interpretation of Scripture. They are usually millenarian, influenced by PENTECOSTALISM and distrustful of organized or institutional Christianity. They believe they are returning to the structures and faith of the first-generation Christians, who built the Church after the death of Christ.

Jesus Prayer 'Lord Jesus Christ have mercy upon me.' A meditative prayer chanted in the Eastern ORTHODOX CHURCH, sometimes in rhythm with the breath and used as a mystical technique to achieve greater closeness to God.

John, Epistles of Three books of the NEW TESTAMENT traditionally ascribed to JOHN, the APOSTLE of Jesus, but probably written by the unknown author of St John's Gospel. The first EPISTLE was written in response to the activities of certain leaders who had separated themselves from the early Church and were promoting a form of GNOSTICISM. The other two epistles are real letters, the first of which deals with similar themes to John 1, while the other is concerned with the correct behaviour of a particular Christian community leader and his lack of hospitality to travelling missionaries and preachers. (*See also* JOHN, GOSPEL OF; REVELATIONS, BOOK OF)

John, Gospel of The fourth GOSPEL, traditionally ascribed to St John, although the actual authorship is not certain. Written later than the three SYNOPTIC GOSPELS, the emphasis is not on the popular teachings of Jesus Christ but on higher doctrinal matters concerning the revelation that Jesus Christ is the Son of God or INCARNATION of the divine. The famous first chapter does not begin with the birth story of Jesus but the proclamation that Jesus is the pre-existent LOGOS who shares in the glory of the Father and demonstrates that glory to the world. The gospel is very selective of the events in Jesus' life and sets most of the action in JERUSALEM rather than GALILEE. Scholarship has usually argued that the gospel is influenced by Greek ideas and mystery religions, although recently there have been attempts to reclaim its Jewish background. It is, however, more contemplative and mystical than the other gospels and has been used as inspiration by contemplatives and mystics of all traditions, not only Christian (*See also* JOHN, ST)

John, St One of the twelve original APOSTLES chosen by Jesus Christ as companions and missionaries. He was a son of Zebedee, a Galilean fisherman, and together with his brother JAMES, and PETER, he belonged to an inner group of disciples chosen to witness the raising of Jairus' daughter and the TRANSFIGURATION. John is certainly the disciple referred to as 'the disciple who Jesus loved' and who was entrusted with the care of MARY after the death of Jesus. He was the first to understand the significance of the missing body when he visited the tomb with Peter on EASTER morning. It is, however, not certain that he was the author of the fourth gospel which carries his name. (*See also* JOHN, GOSPEL OF)

John the Baptist The son of ZACHARIAH and Elizabeth, whose birth was foretold by the angel GABRIEL. He lived as an ascetic in the Judean desert and preached and baptized at the River JORDAN, where he called upon people to repent. He saw his prophetic mission as preparing the way for the coming of the MESSIAH. Recently he has been associated with the ESSENES in QUMRAN but if this is correct, his solitude and new individual mission suggest that he subsequently parted company with the Jewish sect. Christ chose to be baptized by him and according to the NEW TESTAMENT was hailed as the expected Messiah; later, however, whilst in prison, John does not seem to be aware of this when told of Jesus' activities. John attracted the animosity of Herod Antipas who suspected him of being a leader of a rebellious mass movement. He was also unpopular with Herod's wife Herodius, as he had denounced their marriage as illicit. John was consequently imprisoned and killed. In Christianity he is important as the forerunner of Christ and the last of the Jewish prophetic tradition.

Jordan The river which flows from the Sea of Galilee to the Dead Sea in Israel. The river is mentioned throughout the Jewish Scriptures and has become a symbol of purity for Christians. JOHN THE BAPTIST preached and baptized in the Jordan prior to the mission of Jesus, and it here that he baptized Jesus and heralded the coming of the MESSIAH.

Joseph The husband of MARY (the mother of Jesus Christ) and a carpenter by profession. The Gospel writers depict Joseph as a pious Jew and MATTHEW claims that he was descended from the House of DAVID. Jesus was raised by him in NAZARETH and Joseph acted as a father but both Matthew and LUKE make it clear that Jesus was conceived by the HOLY SPIRIT when Joseph and Mary were only betrothed and she was still a virgin. The Gospels refer to other children belonging to the couple and it is natural to assume that they were born after Jesus; however, Roman Catholicism insists that Mary died a virgin. (*See also* JAMES, ST)

Joseph of Arimathea   A pious Jew who was searching for the Kingdom of God and met with Jesus. It is believed that he was a secret Christian and a member of the SANHEDRIN, the Jewish council that voted to kill Jesus. After Jesus' CRUCIFIXION, Joseph offered his tomb for the burial and it was from here that Christ rose from the dead. In Britain, a legend states that he founded the first Christian community in Glastonbury in 63 CE. Other legends claim that he brought Jesus to Britain as a child. (*See also* RESURRECTION)

Judas Iscariot   One of the original twelve APOSTLES chosen by Jesus Christ as companions and missionaries and infamous as the betrayer of Jesus' whereabouts to the Jewish authorities, which led to the trial and CRUCIFIXION of Jesus. Judas was the treasurer for the bands of disciples, and the GOSPEL writers generally depict him as dishonest or full of avarice. Not only does he betray Christ for 30 pieces of silver to the Jewish high priests, but he also objects to MARY anointing the feet of Christ with perfumed ointment, on the grounds that the ointment was expensive. The secret that Judas apparently gave away to the Jewish authorities was the whereabouts of Jesus in the garden of GETHSEMANE after the gathering together of Jesus and the APOSTLES to celebrate the PASSOVER meal. The narrative accounts of the NEW TESTAMENT indicate that he committed suicide on the land that he purchased with the reward of his betrayal. It is difficult to establish why Judas betrayed Christ but he may have been disappointed in his expectations of Jesus as the Jewish MESSIAH who would lead a successful uprising against Rome and restore Israel to greatness.

Jude, St   One of the original twelve apostles chosen by Jesus Christ as his companions and missionaries. He is usually identified with the writer of the Epistle of St Jude. Here the writer identifies himself as the brother of JAMES and therefore he may have been one of the brothers of Jesus Christ. In Roman Catholicism he is regarded as the saint to be invoked in times of great adversity.

Judgement Day *See* PAROUSIA.

Justification The process by which a person passes from a state of SIN to being declared saved by entering into a relationship with God. In Chistianity, the debate was concerned with what an individual had to do in order to be saved. In Protestant theology justification is by REPENTANCE and FAITH in Jesus Christ. In Roman Catholic theology there is more emphasis on GRACE mediated through the SACRAMENTS. St PAUL made justification the central plank of his SOTERIOLOGY. He defines justification as 'God's act of remitting the sins of guilty men, and accounting them righteous, freely, by His grace, through faith in Christ, on the ground, not of their own works, but of the representative law-keeping and redemptive blood-shedding of the Lord Jesus Christ on their behalf'. Debate has taken place between Roman Catholic and Protestant theologians as to whether the emphasis on salvation should lie in justification by faith or justification by works.

K

Kerygma *Lit. preaching.* The proclamation of the good news concerning the offer of salvation brought about by the life, death and RESURRECTION of Jesus Christ which was proclaimed by the early Christians. (*See also* GOSPEL)

Kingdom of God Jesus' teachings concerning the kingdom of God are based on the Jewish idea of a God that rules eternally in heaven but does not yet have full control on Earth. Consequently, the DISCIPLES saw Jesus as the fulfilment of the prophecy that God's kingdom would be established on Earth. However, Jesus modified the teaching to stress the ethical and spiritual qualities that were demanded to enter the kingdom of God rather than offering tangible rewards. The Church has developed a doctrine of an imminent and full manifestation of the kingdom of God that is linked with the second coming of Christ.

Kirk The term used for a PRESBYTERIAN church and the lowest level of authority at which a Presbyterian council will function. (*See also* PRESBYTER)

Kiss of Peace The greeting in the EUCHARIST, also known as Pax, where the participants express their mutual love and unity by a kiss, an embrace or the more formal shaking of hands.

Knox, John (1513–1572) A Scottish Protestant reformer who fled England during the Catholic reign of Queen Mary. He passed his exile in Geneva, where he was influenced by CALVINISM. After returning to Scotland in 1559, he established committees which abolished the authority of the POPE and forbade attendance at Mass. He is the founder of Scottish Presbyterianism. (*See also* CALVIN, JOHN; PRESBYTERIAN; REFORMATION)

Kornvoschinian   A knotted cord used by the Eastern ORTHODOX CHURCH that has the same function as a ROSARY.

Kyrie   *Lit. O Lord.* A title addressed to Jesus in prayer and the diminutive for the KYRIE ELEISON.

Kyrie Eleison   *Lit. Lord, have mercy.* A liturgical prayer addressed to Christ and chanted by the congregation near the beginning of the MASS in response to a series of prayer bids known as the LITANY.

L

Lady Chapel A CHAPEL dedicated to MARY often found at the side of the NAVE in an Anglican or Roman Catholic church.

Lady Day The feast held on 25 March known as the Annunciation of MARY. It celebrates the announcement by the angel GABRIEL of the birth of Jesus and his conception in his mother's womb. Christianity has traditionally believed that Jesus died on the same day that he was conceived, as these two events are the most important in the salvation of the world. (*See also* CHRISTMAS; EASTER; IMMACULATE CONCEPTION)

Lady, Our A common title used by Roman Catholics for MARY, the mother of Jesus.

Laity Members of the church who are not CLERGY or ordained into the priesthood. Most members of monastic orders are laity and those Protestant DENOMINATIONS who do not accept the EPISCOPACY have no priesthood. Their MINISTERS are therefore technically laity. (*See also* BISHOP; PRIEST)

Lamb of God An expression used in the NEW TESTAMENT and first attributed to JOHN THE BAPTIST who described Jesus Christ as the Lamb of God when he came for BAPTISM. The term 'lamb' probably refers to the PASCHAL LAMB, which Jews offered as a sacrifice to the TEMPLE, and which therefore symbolizes the sacrificial role and the removal of sins associated with Jesus Christ in Christian DOCTRINE. (*See also* CRUCIFIXION; REDEMPTION; SIN)

Last Judgement   Christianity, like Judaism, has a strong belief in a personal, merciful God who actively intervenes in human history, with both compassion and wrath, to deliver human beings and punish evil. The NEW TESTAMENT focuses on a future and final judgement that will manifest at the end of time with the triumphant Christ returning to separate the saved from the damned. (*See also* JUSTIFICATION; REDEMPTION; RESURRECTION; ORIGINAL SIN; SIN)

Last Supper   The final meal taken by Christ with his disciples before the CRUCIFIXION described in the GOSPELS. It is believed to have been held on the Jewish feast of the Passover as it reproduces many of the elements of the Passover meal. During the meal, Jesus announced that he would be betrayed by one of the people present in the room. He then performed the action of breaking bread and tasting the wine from a cup and then passing them around the table, stating that they were his body and blood and should be partaken in remembrance of him. Thus the meal is the important precursor for the SACRAMENT of the EUCHARIST.

Lauds   The traditional morning prayer and the first of the divine OFFICES recited by members of the religious orders. Named after the recitation of the Laudate psalms (148–150), it includes PSALMS, hymns, Benedictus and prayers of supplication. (*See also* EVENSONG; MATINS; VESPERS)

Lazarus   A resident of Bethany and the brother of the two sisters Martha and Mary who were friends of Jesus Christ. The NEW TESTAMENT does not tell us anything about Lazarus' background, other than to describe the events of the miracle in which Jesus brought him back to life after he had been pronounced dead for three days. Some commentators have interpreted the story as Jesus foretelling his power over death before his own CRUCIFIXION and RESURRECTION.

Lectern   A stand in a church which supports the Bible and is used for the reading of the LESSON in the various services. Traditionally it is often in the shape of an eagle.

Lectionary   A book containing the list of set scriptural passages and sometimes their extracts which are read throughout the Christian liturgical year in EVENSONG, morning prayer and the EUCHARIST. (*See also* LESSON)

Legate, Papal   A personal representative of the POPE, entrusted with his authority and given important missions on the behalf of the VATICAN. They often function as ambassadors to secular nations. (*See also* NUNCIO)

Lent   The 40 days leading up to EASTER in the Christian cycle of the liturgical year which begin on ASH WEDNESDAY and end on Easter Eve. The 40 days are supposed to be a time of penance and are traditionally observed by fasting or abstinence. Many contemporary Christians will try to give up something that they normally indulge in. Lent was first developed in order to prepare CATECHUMENS for BAPTISM at the Easter vigil.

Lesson   The liturgical reading of the Scripture that takes place in most Christian services. In the Episcopal churches it consists of three readings: one from the OLD TESTAMENT and two from the NEW TESTAMENT. The final reading is from the GOSPELS. Members of the laity are able to make the first two readings but a PRIEST always makes the final reading. In Roman Catholicism and High Church Anglicism, the final reading will be accompanied by incense and a procession of the priest and servers to the LECTERN.

Liberation Theology   Any theology and action that interprets Christian teachings in favour of an oppressed group or identifying an oppressive situation. Thus Feminist or BLACK THEOLOGY can be regarded as a form of Liberation Theology. However, the term is more precisely used for movements begun in South America in the 1960s and 1970s which declared that the Church had often in the past sided with the powerful and the rich instead of the poor and the oppressed. Liberation Theology borrows heavily from Marxist ideology and practice and sees the work of the Church as radical, in that it should work actively to promote social justice and the transformation of society.

Litany   A part of Christian LITURGY first developed in the Eastern churches that aids congregational participation through several short prayers sung by a PRIEST and consisting of a series of petitions which the congregation respond to with a KYRIE ELEISON or 'Lord have mercy'.

Liturgical Movement   Various movements that aimed to restore the active participation of the laity in the official worship of the Church. The modern liturgical movement began in the first decades of the twentieth century amongst certain monastic orders, who were ideally suited for the widening of participation in the LITURGY, as they were primarily concerned with worship and maintained a certain degree of independence from the Church.

Liturgy   The prescribed or formal service of worship performed publicly or communally rather than privately within the various DENOMINA-TIONS of Christianity. Liturgy is also the subject of academic study that aims to assess its origins and development over the last two thousand years. In the Eastern Church, liturgy is the term used for the EUCHARIST. (*See also* EVENSONG; LITURGICAL MOVEMENTS; OFFICE)

Logos   *Lit. word.* Used as a title for Jesus Christ in the fourth Gospel of JOHN. The term 'logos' was used in number of ways in the Greek language, but metaphysically it meant the divine power by which the universe is given unity and coherence. The *logos spermaticus* was the primal word that, like a seed, germinated and gave form to primal matter. Human beings therefore inwardly contain the logos and express it in reason and speech. The most famous use of the term 'logos' in the context of Jesus Christ appears at the beginning of John's Gospel, where the author uses it to refer to the pre-existent word of God incarnated as Jesus Christ.

Lord's Day   *See* SABBATH.

Lord's Prayer   The prayer taught by Jesus to his APOSTLES at the SERMON ON THE MOUNT (Matthew 6.9–13). Christians believe that it is the model of prayer taught by Jesus for all successive generations.

Christian liturgy uses the text of the prayer, which is regarded as particularly sacred in that it expresses Jesus' teaching and is the prayer that he suggested was acceptable to God. The words are as follows:

Our Father in heaven
Hallowed be your name
Your kingdom come
Your will be done
On earth as in heaven.
Give us today our daily bread.
Forgive us our sins
As we forgive those who sin against us.
Lead us not into temptation
But deliver us from evil.
For the kingdom, the power,
And the glory be yours for evermore.
Amen.

Lord's Supper   *See* EUCHARIST.

Love   The greatest of the three theological virtues expounded by PAUL. The NEW TESTAMENT uses the Greek AGAPE, which means the highest form of love that sees something infinitely precious in its object. The highest manifestation of the love of God, according to the APOSTLE, was the birth, life and death of Jesus Christ, and Jesus is the focal point of Christian love. Christ is also the beloved of God and the love between them existed before creation and expresses the innermost nature of the Godhead. Thus Christians believe love is the essential nature of God and it is also the correct and ultimate response of humans towards God. (*See also* FAITH; HOPE)

Low Church   The wing of the CHURCH OF ENGLAND which represents the Protestant tradition, as opposed to HIGH CHURCH, and gives relatively little importance to the priesthood and the SACRAMENTS. (*See also* OXFORD MOVEMENT; TRACTARIANISM)

Loyola, Ignatius   (1491–1556) A major Roman Catholic figure of the REFORMATION period. He was born of a knightly family in Spain and served as a soldier. He retired from military service after receiving injuries and began to read about the lives of the SAINTS. Determined to become a soldier of Christ and the Virgin MARY, he renounced his weapons and dressed as a beggar. He then passed a year in the town of Manresa practising harsh PENANCES and meditating on *The Imitation of Christ* by Thomas à Kempis. During this time he received a number of visions and experiences of ecstasy. After educating himself and practising his own spiritual exercises, recorded in his book, *Spiritual Exercise*, he was inspired to start a monastic order dedicated to the service of the POPE. Ten companions joined him and in 1540, the Pope officially authorized the Society of Jesus, commonly known as the JESUITS. By the 1550s they had been entrusted with the task of combating Protestantism.

Lucifer *Lit. light-bearer.* The Latin name for the planet Venus but also applied to the King of Babylon, who identified himself with the gods. It is used as a synonym for the Devil in which he is described as a fallen angel. This may arise from the idea of fallen pride associated with the King of Babylon. The Book of REVELATION states that the title should be given to Jesus Christ after his ASCENSION and return to God in glory. (*See also* SATAN)

Luke, Gospel of One of the three SYNOPTIC GOSPELS which tell of the birth, life and death of Jesus Christ and which, along with St JOHN's Gospel, form the first four books of the NEW TESTAMENT. It was certainly written by the same author as ACTS OF THE APOSTLES and was probably the same Luke who was the companion and friend of PAUL. The gospel's content suggests that the author had access to eyewitness accounts of the ministry of Jesus as well as previous written sources. The gospel includes most of MARK's gospel and was most certainly derived from the earlier gospel's content. However, it also contains sources drawn from MATTHEW. It is therefore speculated that all three synoptic gospels may have drawn on an earlier source.

Luke, St According to tradition, the writer of the third GOSPEL and the ACTS OF THE APOSTLES. He is believed to have been a physician and a

GENTILE, who accompanied PAUL on some of his missionary journeys (*See also* LUKE, GOSPEL OF)

Luther, Martin   (1483–1546). German Protestant reformer and key figure in the REFORMATION. Luther was an Augustinian monk who broke from the Roman Catholic Church initially over the matter of indulgences. As a Professor of Biblical Studies at the University of Wittenberg, he had already begun to reconsider the Church's DOCTRINES concerning JUSTIFICATION. In 1517, he published his famous 'Ninety-Five Theses on Indulgences' and went on to criticize scholasticism. In 1520, he began to argue forcibly for the reform of the Roman Catholic Church, insisting that it had departed from the teachings of the NEW TESTAMENT. He further developed these arguments by stating that the Church had made the GOSPELS their servant by binding in them in a complex system of SACRAMENTS and priesthood. He left the Augustinian order and married in 1525. (*See also* CALVIN, JOHN; LUTHERANISM; ZWINGLI, ULRICH)

Lutheranism   The religious ideas developed from the thoughts of Martin LUTHER and encapsulated in the Lutheran Church, a Protestant DENOMINATION which is strong in Germany, Scandinavia and the United States. The DOCTRINES of Lutheranism are expressed in the Lesser Catechism (1529) and the Augsberg Confession (1530). While these do not overtly challenge many of the doctrines of Roman Catholicism, they do insist on JUSTIFICATION by FAITH as the correct doctrine based on the teachings of St PAUL. They also condemn the intercession of SAINTS, monastic vows and prescribed fasting, but do not mention the more controversial issues of the priesthood of all believers, TRANSUBSTANTIATION and PURGATORY (*See also* REFORMATION).

Madonna   *Lit. my lady.* A term used for MARY, the mother of Jesus, especially to indicate her statues or icons. (*See also* IMMACULATE CONCEPTION; LADY, OUR)

Magi   *Lit. wise men.* Three wise men who supposedly came from the East under the guidance of a star to offer the newly born Jesus Christ gifts of frankincense, gold and myrrh. Various traditions suggest that they were either kings or Zoroastrian sages. They are symbolically important as they were the first GENTILES or non-Jews to worship Jesus Christ and thus pre-empted the belief that he was a universal saviour rather than the Jewish MESSIAH. (*See also* CHRISTMAS)

Magnificat   The song of praise sung by MARY when she was greeted by her cousin Elizabeth as the mother of the Lord and contained in the first chapter of the GOSPEL of LUKE. It is an integral part of Christian liturgy and sung in EVENSONG or VESPERS in the Western Church. It is part of morning worship in the Eastern churches. It has become an unofficial anthem of South American LIBERATION THEOLOGY because of the implicit bias for the poor and lowly in its words:

My soul proclaims the greatness of the Lord;
My spirit rejoices in God my saviour;
For He has looked with favour on his lowly servant:
From this day all generations will call me blessed;
The Almighty has done great things for me: and holy is His name.
He has mercy on those that fear Him: in every generation.

He has filled the hungry with good things: and the rich He has sent away empty.

He has come to the help of His servant Israel: for He has remembered His promise of mercy,

The Promise He made to our fathers: to Abraham and his children forever.

Mar Thoma   A Christian community in Kerala, south India, who claim that they were founded by the APOSTLE THOMAS but whose earliest existence dates to the sixth century. The oldest Christian presence in India, originally they were NESTORIANS of Syrian origin but in 1599 they united with the Roman Catholic Church. They recognize the Syrian Orthodox Patriarch of Damascus as their leader.

Mariology   The academic study of MARY, the mother of Jesus, and her place in the divine order.

Mark, Gospel of   One of the three SYNOPTIC GOSPELS which, along with St JOHN's Gospel, form the first four books of the NEW TESTAMENT. Its authorship is ascribed to John MARK of JERUSALEM, who was companion of PETER, BARNABAS and PAUL. Many scholars believe it to be the forerunner of the other two Synoptic Gospels, and the forerunner of the GOSPEL style of writing. It is likely that Mark wrote down Peter's memories of the time he spent with Jesus Christ whilst Mark and Peter were travelling and staying in Rome. (*See also* LUKE, GOSPEL OF; MATTHEW, GOSPEL OF)

Mark, St   The traditionally ascribed writer of St Mark's Gospel and early Christian evangelist who travelled with BARNABAS and PAUL. He is also believed to have been in Rome with PETER and Paul. (*See also* MARK, GOSPEL OF)

Martyr   *Lit. witness.* The term used for Christians who have suffered death through persecution. They are often venerated and regarded as intercessors as a result of their conviction that paying the price of the ultimate renunciation of their mortal life was not equal to giving up their life in Christ. This unique reverence for those who had given up their lives for their faith during the persecutions under the Roman authorities began in the second and third centuries of Christianity. By the fourth century it had blossomed into a cult of martyrs, which maintained that the martyrs were not dead but SAINTS living in the presence of the Lord. Their physical remains were often commemorated by special memorials. (*See also* FERETORY; RELICS).

Martyriology   The official register of Christian MARTYRS which contain the names, places of death, commemorative feast days and brief events from their lives. The most famous example is attributed to Usuard and forms the basis for the Roman Catholic martyriology.

Mary Magdelene, St   A follower of Jesus traditionally believed to have been a prostitute before he cast seven devils out of her, and who accompanied him on his evangelistic mission along with the twelve APOSTLES. She was one of the women who found Christ's empty tomb and, according to the Gospel of JOHN, the first person granted an appearance of the resurrected Christ. (*See also* RESURRECTION)

Mary, the Blessed Virgin   The honorific title given to the mother of Christ. The idea of her perpetual virginity was accepted from the fifth century onwards and is first mentioned in the apocryphal Book of JAMES. The GOSPELS themselves say little about Mary other than the birth stories and her presence at Jesus' CRUCIFIXION, when she accompanied 'the disciple that Jesus loved' at the foot of the cross. The ACTS OF THE APOSTLES states that she was devoted to prayer along with the other DISCIPLES. However, the gaps in the gospel accounts are filled by hagiography arising from the beliefs of pious Christians over the ages. (*See also* IMMACULATE CONCEPTION; MAGNIFICAT; VIRGIN BIRTH)

Mass   A term for the EUCHARIST most commonly used by the Roman Catholic Church.

Matins   The designation for the service of morning prayer in the CHURCH OF ENGLAND. Traditionally the first OFFICE of the day, it took place in the early hours of the morning and not long after midnight.

After the REFORMATION, the Protestant churches created a morning prayer service by merging matins and PRIME. The structure of the service is similar to EVENSONG. In monastic communities in the West, matins remains the early morning prayer and consists of a hymn, PSALMS, LESSONS, the Te Deum and a collect.

Matthew, Gospel of   One of the three SYNOPTIC GOSPELS which, along with St JOHN's Gospel, form the first four books of the NEW TESTAMENT and recount the birth, life and death of Jesus Christ. It is more concerned with the relationship between the ethical teachings of Jesus and Jewish law than the other GOSPELS. There has been controversy over its authorship, as it contains almost the complete Gospel of MARK, who was not one of the original APOSTLES. Scholars have debated the question of why an original eyewitness of Jesus Christ's life would rely on the account of someone who was not there in person. However, the writer of Matthew does include a large number of sayings of Jesus taken from a source that seems to be common with the author of LUKE's Gospel. (*See also* LUKE, GOSPEL OF; MARK, GOSPEL OF)

Matthew, St   One of the original twelve APOSTLES, who were chosen by Jesus Christ as his companions and first missionaries, and traditionally believed to be the writer of the first GOSPEL. He is believed to have been a tax-collector and his gospel recounts how Jesus entered the tax office and declared that Matthew should leave and follow him. (*See also* MATTHEW, GOSPEL OF)

Matthias, St   The APOSTLE chosen to replace JUDAS ISCARIOT after his betrayal of Jesus Christ and subsequent suicide and to bring the number back to twelve. Little is known of Matthias' later career as an apostle although GNOSTIC groups claimed to have secret teachings that originated from him and there are apocryphal works attributed to him.

Maundy Thursday   The day in the Christian liturgical year which is celebrated on the Thursday before EASTER. It commemorates the LAST SUPPER and has traditionally been used to bless holy oils. The night of Maundy Thursday is also marked by vigils to remember the prayer vigil demanded by Jesus Christ of his DISCIPLES in the garden of GETHSEMANE. (*See also* CHRISM; GOOD FRIDAY)

Meditation   The term used in Christian spirituality to describe a discursive exercise of devout reflection on a passage of Scripture in order to deepen insight and increase devotion.

Mendicant Friars   Members of religious preaching orders who are forbidden to have common property. In the Middle Ages they traditionally begged for a living or even worked. They are not bound to one monastery or under the control of the EPISCOPACY and were given considerable privileges to preach and hear confessions. (*See also* DOMINICANS; FRANCISCANS)

Messiah   *Lit. the anointed one.* The Jews believed that God would send a descendant of DAVID to deliver His people; this expectation was heightened by the Roman occupation and consequently contained both religious and political hope of deliverance. During Jesus' lifetime, there is no doubt that there were expectations of his being the Jewish messiah. In the preaching of the early Church, Jesus is still identified with the Jewish messiah as the deliverer of his people, but after the RESURRECTION, the APOSTLES begin to preach the message that Jesus remains the messiah after his death as he is now enthroned in glory at the right hand of God. Gradually, the messianic hope of the early Christians shifted from the Jewish expectation of a political/religious leader who would fulfil their national hopes to a world messiah who had come to restore all humanity to God. (*See also* ATONEMENT; JESUS CHRIST)

Methodism   A Protestant DENOMINATION which came into existence from the revivalist inspiration of the preaching of John WESLEY (1703–91) against the general moral laxity in the working classes and the rationality of the established CHURCH OF ENGLAND. Initially, Wesley had not wanted to break with the Church of England or establish separate places of worship. However, there were doctrinal differences, and after his death in 1791, the Wesleyan Methodists formed as separate sect of NON-CONFORMIST Christianity. They were named Methodists because of their methodical practice of prayer and Bible study.

Metropolitan   The title given to a BISHOP with provincial rather than diocesan authority who has the rank of ARCHBISHOP or PRIMATE.

Militant, The Church   *See* CHURCH MILITANT, THE.

Millenarianism   Various groups within Christianity who emphasize a belief in an imminent thousand years of peace which will either follow the second coming of Christ or prepare the way for it. Millenarianism has a long history in Christianity which goes back to the early church, some of whose members expected an early return of the resurrected Christ, through to the Protestant Reformation, where it was represented by ANABAPTISTS and groups of brethren. The arrival of the third Christian millennium has revived interest in Millenarianism amongst some movements, but mainstream Christian churches remain cautious. (*See also* ADVENTISTS; PAROUSIA)

Minister   A person who is officially responsible for carrying out religious functions in the church. In NON-CONFORMIST churches it is the usual term used for the CLERGY who are not members of the priesthood as in Roman Catholicism and Anglicanism. (*See also* PRIEST)

Missal   The Roman Catholic book that contains all the text and the directions for performing the MASS. It was first developed in the thirteenth century in order to allow the PRIEST to perform the SACRAMENT alone. (*See also* BREVIARY)

Missions   The propagation of the Christian faith to non-Christian people by preaching the GOSPEL. A primary task of the Church since the origin of Christianity, it became linked with empire and colonialism from the sixteenth century, since when Christian mission has been associated with three world powers: Spain in the sixteenth and seventeenth centuries, Britain in the nineteenth and the USA in the twentieth. Christian mission is becoming aware of the necessity to acknowledge cultural diversity and avoid Western cultural forms when evangelizing. (*See also* APOSTLES; EVANGELICALS)

Monarchianism   A second- and third-century theological movement arising in Byzantium which believed in the unity of the Godhead and played down the idea of the Son as an independent entity. The early form of Monarchianism, developed from the ideas of Theodotus, claimed that Jesus Christ was fully human and therefore not a part of the Godhead. However, the more successful later Monarchianism developed from Noetus. This teaching claimed that it was the Father Himself who was born and there was consequently no independent being known as the Son. (*See also* ARIANISM; CHRISTOLOGY; MONOPHYSITISM; TRINITARIANISM; TRINITY)

Monastery   The house of a religious community containing MONKS, FRIARS or NUNS belonging to one of the Christian ORDERS. (*See also* ABBESS; ABBOT; CONVENT; MENDICANT FRIARS; RELIGIOUS)

Monasticism   The idea of monasticism developed from the early Christian hermits who withdrew from the world and lived in the desert, but had its roots in the Christian MARTYRS who had considered their FAITH to be greater than the values of the world around them. From around the fourth century, monastic communities began to develop in the East and by the end of the century had spread to the West. The basic framework of the movement was based on the idea of progression from BAPTISM into a life in Christ through to a contemplative knowledge of God achieved through renunciation, asceticism, PENANCE, prayer, fasting and service. By the fifth century, the order of St BENEDICT (480–550) had been formed and was to become the norm for all orders of Western monasticism. (*See also* BENEDICTINE; CISTERCIANS; CONVENT; DOMINICANS; FRANCISCANS; MENDICANT FRIARS; MONASTERY; MONK; NUN; RELIGIOUS)

Monk   A member of the laity or priesthood who lives the life of MONASTICISM according to the rule of one of the RELIGIOUS ORDERS in order to achieve personal closeness to God through the vows of poverty, chastity and obedience. (*See also* MONASTERY)

Monophysitism   The fifth-century dissenting DOCTRINE opposed to the views of the Council of Chalcedon (451) that asserts Christ had only one divine nature rather than the ORTHODOX view that he was both fully human and fully divine. It is still prevalent in the eastern Mediterranean, including the Coptic, Armenian, Syrian and Abyssinian churches. (*See also* ARIANISM; CHRISTOLOGY; COUNCIL; EBIONITIES; NICAEA, COUNCIL OF)

Monsignor   A title given in the Roman Catholic Church to a CARDINAL or any other high clerical office that is directly appointed by the POPE. (*See also* PAPACY)

Montanism   A second-century apocalyptic movement founded by Montanus around the year 170 CE and which believed in the imminence of the last days. The movement was known for its moral rigour, asceticism and refusal to compromise with society. Montanus claimed to be a prophet and the movement spread rapidly from Asia Minor to Rome, alarming the leaders of the Christian community. Its greatest convert was Tertullian, a famous early Christian writer. Montanism was eventually condemned at a number of COUNCILS. (*See also* MILLENARIANISM)

Moral Theology   The theological study of Christian behaviour and character first treated systematically by Thomas AQUINAS in the second section of SUMMA THEOLOGICA. In recent years attention has shifted from attempting to find systems of behaviour that are binding on all Christians to treating each case as individual but guided by the overriding principle of LOVE.

Morning Prayer   *See* MATINS.

Mortal Sin   A form of SIN that is a deliberate act of turning away from God. It is committed with clear knowledge of its consequences and full consent of the will. It will bring the punishment of eternal damnation unless repented. (*See also* ACTUAL SIN; ATONEMENT; CONFESSION; ORIGINAL SIN; PENANCE)

N

Name of Jesus St JOHN's Gospel seems to use the idea of belief in the name as synonymous with personal commitment or FAITH in Jesus Christ and generally it is used in the NEW TESTAMENT as reference to Christ's power and authority. The first disciples perform miracles and baptize in the name of Jesus. Devotion to the holy name became popular under the influence of the FRANCISCANS in the fifteenth century. (*See also* BAPTISM)

Natalitia *Lit. birthday*. A term used in the early Church to commemorate the deathdays of MARTYRS in the sense that their death was believed to mask their birth into eternal life. (*See also* SAINTS)

Nathanael One of the original twelve APOSTLES who were chosen by Jesus Christ as his companions and missionaries. Although mentioned in all the NEW TESTAMENT lists of the original twelve, nothing further is known about him. The Gospel of JOHN tells the story of how he came to Jesus through PHILIP but maintained the normal Jewish scepticism towards anyone born in NAZARETH. He was convinced that he had found the Jewish MESSIAH when Jesus knew who he was without formerly meeting him.

Nativity *See* CHRISTMAS.

Nave In traditional CHURCH architecture the nave is the main part of the church which runs from west to east, from the front door to the SANCTUARY, and is assigned to the congregation. (*See also* CHANCEL; ALTAR)

Nazarene   Someone who comes from the town of NAZARETH. Jesus Christ is called 'Jesus the Nazarene' in the NEW TESTAMENT on several occasions. The Galilean people were looked down upon by the Jews of Judea and there may be a note of derision in calling Jesus a Nazarene. The Judean Jews called the first Christians Nazarenes and the Jewish/Christian movements that originated in the JERUSALEM Church may have called themselves Nazarenes.

Nazareth   The town in GALILEE where Christ was raised by MARY and Joseph and lived for around 30 years until rejected by its people. The NEW TESTAMENT indicates that because of his origins he was known as 'Jesus of Nazareth'. (*See also* NAZARENE)

Nestorian   A DOCTRINE attributed to NESTORIUS (fifth century) but probably originating with Theodore, Bishop of Mopsuestia (392–428) concerning the nature of Jesus Christ, which asserts that the divine and human aspects of Christ were independent and separate. This is opposed to ORTHODOX CHRISTOLOGY, which teaches that Christ was simultaneously both fully human and fully divine. After the Council of Ephesus in 431, those BISHOPS who would not accept the orthodox view formed their own Nestorian church, which was centred in Persia. Today, the Syrian ORTHODOX CHURCH still maintains a Nestorian position.

Nestorius   A monk from Antioch who was made Patriarch of Constantinople in 428 and immediately entered the controversy concerning the human and divine nature of Jesus Christ. He maintained the position of Theodore, Bishop of Mopsuestia (392–428), that the two aspects of Christ's nature were independent and distinct. On arrival in the capital of Christendom, he gave a sermon in which he declared 'that which is formed in a womb is not . . . God' but that God was within the human nature of Christ. After 431, Nestorius was defeated by the allies of Cyril, the Patriarch of Alexandria, and retired to his MONASTERY in Antioch. However, the issue created the first division in Christianity. (*See also* NESTORIAN)

New Testament   The collection of 27 books written after the death of Jesus Christ which form the distinctively Christian part of the canon of Scripture known as the BIBLE. The New Testament provides the scriptural affirmation of the new covenant that replaces the old Jewish covenant given to Moses through the salvation offered by FAITH in Jesus Christ. Just as the OLD TESTAMENT records the history of God's revelation through the prophets, the New Testament records the final revelation through the incarnation of the Son of God. The 27 books are divided into the four GOSPELS; the ACTS OF THE APOSTLES; 21 EPISTLES written by the APOSTLES and the Book of REVELATION. Although the earliest books were the letters written by PAUL somewhere between 48 and 60 CE, the order of the New Testament is organized chronologically according to when the events described took place. The central message of the New Testament is salvation: God Himself is the saviour through the mediation of Jesus Christ, and salvation is obtained through God's GRACE calling forth the human response of faith and obedience to God's will.

Nicaea, Council of   The first ecumenical council called by CONSTANTINE, the first Christian emperor of the Roman empire, in 325 to resolve the destabilizing controversies caused by various understandings of Christ's human and divine nature, especially the Arian heresy. The council, composed of members from throughout the Christian world, asserted the ORTHODOX position laid out in the NICENE CREED that Christ is both fully human and fully divine. (*See also* ARIANISM)

Nicene Creed   The fullest version of the CREED which contains strong statements concerning the divinity of Christ and His unity with God such as 'God from God' and 'being of one substance with the Father'. It was compiled to resist a number of CHRISTOLOGICAL HERESIES that existed in the fourth-century Church and to provide believers with a statement of ORTHODOX belief. (*See also* APOSTLES' CREED; NICAEA, COUNCIL OF)

Nicholas, St   The Bishop of Myra who is reputed to have participated in the Council of NICAEA in 325 CE. He is the patron SAINT of sailors, children and Russia. It is in his role as the patron saint of children that he is best known as Santa Claus or Father Christmas. (*See also* CHRISTMAS)

Nicodemus   The devout Jew, described as a PHARISEE and member of the SANHEDRIN, who came to Jesus secretly at night and provoked the famous discourse on spiritual rebirth found in John 3.1–15. He protested against the condemnation of Christ and it is believed that he later helped in the burial of Jesus. (*See also* CRUCIFIXION)

Nihilianism   The DOCTRINE that the human nature of Christ was nothing and that his essential being was contained only in the Godhead. It was condemned as HERESY in the twelfth century. (*See also* CHRISTOLOGY)

Non-conformist   Protestant DENOMINATIONS separated from the CHURCH OF ENGLAND during the period of the Civil War and the Restoration in the seventeenth century. The term is generally used to describe Protestant movements that have broken away from or dissented from the state Church of England. These would include BAPTISTS, English PRESBYTERIANS, CONGREGATIONALISTS and METHODISTS. (*See also* CALVINISM; PURITANS)

Novice   A probationary member of a monastic community who is expected to observe the vows of their ORDER but can leave without incurring any penalty before taking final vows to become a MONK or NUN. (*See also* FRIAR; OBLATE)

Nun   A female member of a monastic community who has undertaken the vows of chastity, poverty and obedience. (*See also* MONK; NOVICE; OBLATE; RELIGIOUS)

Nunc Dimittis   The Song of Simeon from Luke 2.29–32 used in Christian evening LITURGY and funerals. Roman Catholics sing it at COMPLINE, Anglicans at EVENSONG, whereas Eastern ORTHODOX CHURCHES sing it at VESPERS. (*See also* CANTICLE)

Nuncio An ambassador or diplomatic representative of the VATICAN, the independent city-state which is the administrative and ecclesiastical centre of Roman Catholicism and home of the POPE.

Nuptial Mass The Roman Catholic MASS held at weddings which includes the celebration and blessing of the marriage itself. (*See also* SACRAMENT)

O

Obedience   One of three vows undertaken by a RELIGIOUS, a member of a monastic community. Absolute obedience is only due to God, whereas obedience to humans is limited by authority and conscience. Generally, in a monastic community obedience will be maintained through the rules of the individual ORDER.

Oblate   Members of the Laity who live in close connection to a religious or monastic ORDER but do not take the full vows of poverty, chastity and OBEDIENCE. It is often used as preparation for the novitiate into the order but some individuals remain oblates throughout their lives. The term was originally used in the Middle Ages for children offered to the service of God by being dedicated to a MONASTERY and brought up by the MONKS. (*See also* NOVICE; RELIGIOUS)

Oblations   The technical term that is applied both to the offering of the consecrated bread and wine used in the EUCHARIST and to any gift brought by the congregation to the Eucharist service for use by the CLERGY or given to charity.

Offertory   The procession that brings the elements of bread and wine as an offering from the congregation to the PRIEST so that it may be CONSECRATED at the ALTAR and participated in by the communicants at the EUCHARIST. (*See also* HOST)

Office, Divine   The daily prayer, introduced in the fifth century, which is supposed to be performed seven times a day by PRIESTS and

RELIGIOUS. Their arrangement was fixed by St BENEDICT in the sixth century and consists of LAUDS, PRIME, terce, sext, none, VESPERS and COMPLINE. Each office is made up of PSALMS, HYMNS, LESSONS, ANTIPHONS, prayers and responses. At the REFORMATION, Protestant churches replaced them with two daily offices of morning and evening prayer. (*See also* EVENSONG; MATINS)

Office, Occasional   The term used in the Book of Common Prayer to describe offices or prayer-rites which are held on a particular occasion rather than as part of daily worship such as visitation of the sick or BAPTISM. (*See also* OFFICE, DIVINE)

Old Catholics   A collection of small national churches in Holland, Germany, Austria, Switzerland and Croatia that have separated themselves from the Roman Catholic Church after objecting to the doctrine of papal INFALLIBILITY introduced in 1870 at VATICAN COUNCIL I. Ordination is received from the Jansenist church of Utrecht.

Old Testament   The portion of the canon of Scripture which Christians share with Judaism, it consisting of the 39 books of Hebrew Scripture. Christians view the text differently from Jews, in that they see the NEW TESTAMENT as the fulfilment of the Jewish Scriptures. The Old Testament is often used as a prophetic preparation for the coming of Jesus Christ. An Old Testament reading takes place in Christian services and there is also extensive use of the PSALMS in Christian worship.

Olives, Mount of   The highest point of a range of hills just outside the walls of eastern JERUSALEM. The base of the mount contains the garden of GETHSEMANE where Jesus Christ and his DISCIPLES passed the night before his arrest. The Mount of Olives is traditionally believed to be the site of Jesus Christ's ASCENSION into heaven and at the summit there is a Muslim shrine believed to contain Jesus' footprints.

Opus Dei   *Lit. the work of God.* A powerful conservative Roman Catholic organization founded in Spain in 1928 to promote the application of Christian morality to daily living. The organization is traditional Spanish Catholicism at its most conservative and functions to combat liberal Catholicism, particularly LIBERATION THEOLOGY in South America.

Oratory   A term used generically for a place of worship other than the parish church. However, most oratories are more likely to be the place of worship used by the Oratorians, a Roman Catholic congregation of PRIESTS who live in a community but do not take monastic vows of poverty, chastity and obedience. Cardinal Newman introduced them into Britain in 1848.

Order   A monastic community of MONKS, FRIARS or NUNS, such as the FRANCISCANS, DOMINICANS or BENEDICTINES, living under a set rule. Also the division of the priesthood into three hierarchical categories of BISHOP, PRIEST and DEACON. (*See also* CARMELITES)

Orders   The term used for the divine calling or vocation believed to come from God to an individual to be ordained into the priesthood in the Episcopal churches. The sacramental service of ordination into the priesthood is known as the Sacrament of Orders. (*See also* PRIEST; SACRAMENT)

Ordination   The SACRAMENT performed by a BISHOP in the Episcopal churches which provides entry to the priesthood. The service of ordination always takes place in the context of the EUCHARIST and includes the laying on of hands by a bishop and the repetition of a special prayer known as the ordination prayer. Traditionally, the candidate for priesthood was a baptized and confirmed male of good moral character who had felt the vocation from God to be a PRIEST. Recently, the CHURCH OF ENGLAND has joined the rest of the ANGLICAN COMMUNION in extending ordination to women. (*See also* ORDERS)

Orientation   The traditional method of construction used in church architecture that ensures that the longer axis leading up the NAVE to the SANCTUARY always runs from east to west.

Origen (185–254). One of the church fathers and an early influential theologian who provided the foundations for Eastern Christian thought. There are some doubts about his orthodoxy, as he believed that creation was eternal and that the divinity of the Son was somehow less than that of the Father, but he developed the important notion of a distinction between the surface meaning of Scripture and allegorical interpretation, leading to deeper spiritual understanding. He also adopted the theological position of universalism, which asserts that all creatures will eventually be saved by a loving God. (*See also* ARIANISM; ORIGENISM; UNIVERSALISM)

Origenism The group of theological speculations attributed to ORIGEN, in particular the pre-existence of souls and the denial of the identity between the mortal and the resurrected body. Origen's ideas were condemned as heretical at the Council of Alexandria in 400 CE and after a renaisssance in the fifth and sixth centuries were once again refuted at the Second Council of Constantinople in 553 CE.

Original Sin The state of SIN which humankind has inherited from the FALL of ADAM and EVE and which means that all human beings are born in the state of sin and separated from God. Human nature is therefore flawed or corrupted and requires the intervention of God to attain salvation and reconciliation. The theology of original sin was fully developed by St AUGUSTINE OF HIPPO in the fourth and fifth centuries CE and came under considerable criticism from Enlightenment thinkers who saw it as an obstacle to social and political development. In ORTHODOX Christian tradition, infant BAPTISM is perceived as the remission of the inheritance of original sin. (*See also* PELAGIANS)

Orthodox The term used to define right belief as opposed to HERESY. Generally debates concerning right doctrine took place at a series of COUNCILS. Those adhering to non-orthodox belief were likely to find themselves treated as sects and even EXCOMMUNICATED from the Church. However, since the rise of DENOMINATIONS, orthodoxy is more likely to describe conformity to the CREEDS sanctioned by the ecumenical councils.

Orthodox Church   The appellation for the Eastern Church, which is formed of several independent national churches which include the original Eastern patriarchates who are in communion with the patriarchate of Constantinople. The Orthodox church developed from the Christianity of the Byzantine Empire but gradually became independent churches with the rise of nation states in Europe. The Byzantine Church had experienced its first schism arising from MONOPHYSITE and NESTORIAN disputes in the fifth and sixth centuries but a greater split occurred with the separation of Christianity into the Orthodox and Roman Catholic Churches in 1054. The Orthodox churches believe in seven SACRAMENTS or 'mysteries', BAPTISM is by full immersion and children participate in Communion from a young age. The most distinctive aspects of Orthodoxy are the LITURGY and the extensive use of ICONS. Monastic communities are influential and although parish PRIESTS are allowed to marry, BISHOPS are selected from the monastic communities.

Oxford Movement   An Anglican movement of the nineteenth century determined to restore HIGH CHURCH principles and which began in Oxford. The leaders were John Henry Newman (1801–90), Richard Froude (1803–36) Edward Pusey (1880–82) and John Keble (1792–1866). In spite of some conversions to Roman Catholicism, most notably John Newman, the majority stayed in the CHURCH OF ENGLAND, where they had considerable influence on LITURGY and ceremonial. They were also responsible for the restoration of monastic life to the Church of England. (*See also* TRACTARIANISM)

P

Padre   A popular designation of a CHAPLAIN to the armed forces. It is sometimes used to describe a PRIEST.

Pall   A cloth that is spread over a coffin at a funeral but also used to describe the small cloth that covers the CHALICE at the EUCHARIST.

Palm Sunday   The Sunday before EASTER which celebrates Christ's triumphant entry into JERUSALEM. Often the worship will be accompanied by a procession around the outside or the inside of the church.

Papacy   The doctrinal and administrative office of the POPE which is the central organization and leadership of the Roman Catholic Church. The authority of the Pope is believed to derive from the apostle PETER who led the Roman Church before his martyrdom. Catholicism maintains that Peter was the first Pope and that there is unbroken line to the present day. (*See also* APOSTOLIC SUCCESSION; CARDINAL; COLLEGE; INFALLIBILITY; VATICAN)

Parables   *Lit. putting things side by side.* The allegorical teaching or the utilization of analogy that Jesus Christ used to convey spiritual truths. Many parables are attributed to Jesus in the GOSPEL accounts and they usually recount short descriptive stories or develop similes in order to illustrate a single truth or answer a question.

Paraclete   *See* HOLY SPIRIT.

Paradise   *See* HEAVEN.

Pardon   *See* INDULGENCES.

Parish   An ecclesiastical, pastoral and administrative area under the control of a member of the CHURCH OF ENGLAND CLERGY. Several parishes will form one DIOCESE under the control of a BISHOP. All the inhabitants of that area are entitled to his/her spiritual care and assistance. (*See also* INCUMBENT; VICAR)

Parousia   *Lit. presence or arrival.* The expected return or the second coming of Jesus Christ in which he will announce the last days and the final judgement by God of humanity. According to the Book of REVELATION this will be marked by a gigantic struggle between the forces of good and evil and a series of portents, natural disasters, plagues and wars. In the final confrontation between Christ and the forces of SATAN, Christ will triumph and herald a thousand years of peace and righteousness. (*See also* ARMAGEDDON)

Parson   Sometimes used in the CHURCH OF ENGLAND to describe any member of the CLERGY but originally it had the same meaning as rector – that is, a clergyman who had full rights over a benefice. (*See also* PRIEST; VICAR)

Paschal   Referring to the Jewish Passover or EASTER.

Paschal Lamb   The lamb sacrificed at the Jewish feast of Passover and by analogy used to refer to Christ's sacrificial role remembered at EASTER. (*See also* LAMB OF GOD)

Passion   The redemptive suffering of Jesus Christ which took place in the final week of his life and is celebrated in the Christian festival of EASTER. (*See also* ATONEMENT; CRUCIFIXION; HOLY WEEK; REDEMPTION; RESURRECTION)

Paten   The dish which holds the bread during the EUCHARIST. (*See also* CHALICE; HOST)

Paternoster   The Latin title of the LORD'S PRAYER which is taken from the first two words, 'Our Father'.

Patriarch   The title given to the heads of the various Eastern ORTHODOX CHURCHES which is derived from the old title used for the BISHOPS of the five principal SEES in the Christian world. The Patriarch of Constantinople is regarded as the titular head but each patriarch is the actual leader of a nationally autonomous church within ORTHODOXY.

Patristics   The period of the church fathers lasting from 100 to 451 CE, or the theological study of their writings and the distinctive DOCTRINES that developed in their period, especially regarding CHRISTOLOGY.

Patron saint   A SAINT who has been chosen as the intercessor or guardian of a particular person, organization, or place.

Paul, St   The APOSTLE who was most influential in the development of early Christianity through spreading the message of Jesus to the GENTILES. Born a Jew and possibly brought up as a PHARISEE in Tarsus, he had initially fiercely opposed the first Christians and was present as a sympathizer at the stoning of STEPHEN, the first Christian MARTYR. After seeing a vision of the risen Christ on the road to Damascus, he converted to Christianity. He believed that Jewish law should not be imposed on non-Jewish Christians and embarked on a number of missionary tours around the Mediterranean world culminating in his visit to Rome, where he was imprisoned for two years. Paul's contribution to the development of Christianity is documented in the ACTS OF THE APOSTLES and he wrote a number of EPISTLES to several of the early Christian communities to inspire their FAITH, resolve their problems and correct doctrinal errors. These form some of the earliest contributions to the NEW TESTAMENT. (*See also* COLOSSIANS; CORINTHIANS; EPHESIANS; PHILIPPIANS; ROMANS; TIMOTHY AND TITUS)

Pax   *See* KISS OF PEACE.

Peculiar   An ecclesiastical centre in the CHURCH OF ENGLAND, which is not under the authority of the BISHOP in charge of the DIOCESE. The two notable peculiars in Britain are WESTMINSTER ABBEY and St George's Chapel in WINDSOR which are both under the direct authority of the sovereign.

Pelagians   Followers of the British monk Pelagius, based in Rome, who opposed the DOCTRINE of ORIGINAL SIN and PREDESTINATION as taught by St AUGUSTINE OF HIPPO. Pelagius argued that human beings have complete free will and the power to reject or accept the GOSPEL without the added weight of original sin to contend with. He used GRACE to signify the natural human capacities already given by God which, if used effectively, are sufficient to save humanity from SIN.

Penal substitution   A Protestant DOCTRINE that Christ was the sinless victim punished in the place of sinful humanity. Thus he was a substitute who sacrificed his own self as ATONEMENT for those who had been elected by God for salvation. (*See also* REDEMPTION; SATIS-FACTION)

Penance   One of the seven SACRAMENTS recognized by the Roman Catholic Church. The PENANCE is given by the PRIEST, known as a penitentiary, at CONFESSION before the pronouncement of ABSOLUTION.

Penitentiary   *See* PENANCE.

Pentecost   The festival that commemorates the day when the APOSTLES received the gift of the HOLY SPIRIT and spoke in tongues. After this occasion, which is described in the ACTS OF THE APOSTLES, they began to preach and perform miracles in the name of Jesus. The festival is also known as Whitsun and takes place in May on the Sunday which falls on the final or fiftieth day of EASTER. (*See also* GLOSSOLALIA; PENTECOSTALISTS)

Pentecostalists   A modern religious movement which received its impetus from a series of revivalist meetings led by the black preacher William Seymour (d. 1923) at Los Angeles in 1906. The movement, which is now interdenominational, believes it is possible for Christians to receive the same experience as the APOSTLES during the original Pentecostal event. They give particular emphasis to GLOSSO-LALIA, prophecy, healing and exorcism. There are specific Pentecostal churches which flourish amongst the African-Caribbean migrant communities in Britain and other black-led churches. The Pentecostal churches that call themselves the Assemblies of God are predominantly white, whereas the Churches of God in Christ are mainly black. The movement is now spreading to many parts of the world and can be found in North and South America, Asia, Africa and Europe. (*See also* PENTECOST)

Peter, Epistles of St   There are two letters ascribed to St PETER which are included in the books of the NEW TESTAMENT. Addressing a wide audience, the first dwells upon the themes of persecution, whilst the second is concerned with refuting false teachers. There is more doubt concerning the authorship of the second EPISTLE, as the style of language is different from the first. Peter's contribution to the New Testament goes beyond the two epistles, as it is likely that MARK based his Gospel on Peter's first-hand accounts of travelling with Jesus Christ. (*See also* MARK, EPISTLE OF)

Peter, St   A Galilean fisherman and one of the original twelve APOSTLES who were chosen by Jesus Christ as his companions and first missionaries, and regarded as the foremost amongst their number. He is known as the Prince of the Apostles and his name is always written first in any list of Jesus' original DISCIPLES. He is believed to be buried in St Peter's in Rome where he probably died during the persecution of Christians by Nero. The Roman Catholic Church regards him as the first POPE, based on the belief that he was the first BISHOP of Rome. His original name was Simon and it is believed that Jesus renamed him Peter (*petros* – a rock). He was present at the TRANS-FIGURATION and although famous for three denials of Christ at the time of the CRUCIFIXION, he undertook the leadership of the disciples after Jesus' ASCENSION. He was instrumental in bringing the message of Jesus to non-Jews and after several missionary tours helped develop the fledgling church in Rome. (*See also* PETER, EPISTLE OF)

Pew   Fixed wooden benches known as pews were probably introduced into the NAVE of Western churches sometime in the medieval period as a concession to the old and sick, but are now the usual form of seating for the congregation.

Pharisees   The founders of rabbinical Judaism and strict upholders of the Torah who were criticized by Jesus for their purely external conformity to the law and subsequent self-righteousness. (*See also* SADDUCEES)

Philemon, Epistle to   A letter written by PAUL whilst imprisoned, requesting the release of a Christian, Onesimus, from his owner, Philemon. Onesimus had been converted by Paul after meeting the APOSTLE in prison.

Philip   One of the original twelve APOSTLES who were chosen by Jesus Christ as his companions and first missionaries. He was from the town of Bethsaida and is placed fifth amongst the twelve in the GOSPEL lists of the DISCIPLES. He is mentioned in the NEW TESTAMENT on three occasions. He asks Jesus if he can have a vision of the Father; brings Greeks to him; and expresses his inability to deal with the lack of food before the miracle of the feeding of the five thousand.

Philippians, Epistle to the   One of the books of the NEW TESTAMENT, which consists of the letter of PAUL to the church in Philippi which he had established as the first Christian community in Europe. It refers to Paul's imprisonment and was probably written during his two-year spell of captivity in Rome. The purpose of the letter seems to have been to introduce TIMOTHY to the church as a future missionary. While Paul does address some doctrinal issues and a rebuttal of GNOSTIC influence, on the whole the tone of the letter is one of personal exhortation and encouragement, outlining Paul's own hopes for himself and his future plans.

Plainsong   The traditional liturgical music of the Roman Catholic MASS, also known as the Gregorian chant, which does not require any accompaniment by a musical instrument. It is rarely used since the liturgical changes of VATICAN COUNCIL II, except by some monastic orders.

Pontifex Maximus   *Lit. the supreme priest.* One of the titles of the POPE.

Pontifical   The prayer book used in the Western Church which contains the prayers and ceremonies for rites performed by a BISHOP such as CONFIRMATION and ORDINATION. A revised edition was produced by the Roman Catholic Church at the VATICAN COUNCIL II in 1962.

Pontius Pilate   The fifth Roman Governor (*praefectus*) of Judea who presided over the CRUCIFIXION of Christ. The NEW TESTAMENT seems to indicate that he was more concerned with displeasing the emperor through the possibility of unrest in Judea than pleasing the SANHEDRIN, whose decisions he had the power to overrule. (*See also* BARABBAS)

Poor Clares   A strict and austere enclosed contemplative ORDER of NUNS founded by St CLARE (1194–1253) and St FRANCIS as the female branch of the FRANCISCANS sometime between 1212 and 1214. Their nunnery at the church of St Damion in Assisi was the only one founded by St Francis himself, although others were founded in central Italy soon after the saint's death.

Pope   The title given to the chief BISHOP of the Roman Catholic Church. (*See also* PAPACY)

Popery   A Protestant term of hostility towards the DOCTRINES and practices of the Roman Catholic Church. (*See also* PAPACY; POPE)

Postulant   The preliminary stage of being tested before becoming a novitiate of a RELIGIOUS or monastic ORDER. (*See also* NOVICE)

Prayer   Christian prayer shares with other world religions prayers of petition, adoration, invocation, thanksgiving and penitence. Prayer may be offered in private individual devotion or in set liturgical forms which are congregational. Prayer may also be vocal or silent.

In silent prayer the individual attempts to ascend mentally and emotionally to God, and various disciplines have been developed by the monastic ORDERS to help achieve this. This has given rise to a number of Christian mystics. The distinct aspects of Christian prayer arise from the atoning role of Jesus Christ, who provides the deepest evidence of the personal and intimate relationship which God has with His creation. It is Christ who has provided the JUSTIFICATION that makes it possibile to come close to God and many prayers are made through his intercession. (*See also* ATONEMENT; EUCHARIST; EVENSONG; LITURGY; LORD'S PRAYER; MATINS; MEDITATION; OFFICE, DIVINE)

Predestination   The doctrine, usually associated with John CALVIN, which asserts that God in his omniscience has determined the fate of all creatures, and therefore eternal damnation or eternal reward has already been decided for each individual. While the problem of predestination arises out of free-will and omnipotence, St AUGUSTINE OF HIPPO saw it as a matter of GRACE. He argued that salvation does not come as a reward for good actions, as all human beings are under the sway of SIN. Only grace can set human beings free but grace is not given to everybody, therefore only some were predestined to be saved. The doctrine of predestination remains associated with movements that arose out of CALVINISM. (*See also* ORIGINAL SIN; PRESBYTERIANS)

Prelate   A term used for members of the CLERGY who have attained high rank. In the CHURCH OF ENGLAND it is reserved for BISHOPS. (*See also* ARCHBISHOP; CARDINAL; POPE)

Presbyter   The elders of the PRESBYTERIAN churches modelled upon the earliest form of Christian organization in Palestine that was in turn based upon the Jewish synagogues. (*See also* PRESBYTERY)

Presbyterian   The churches established from the DOCTRINES of John CALVIN and based upon his model of organization imposed in Geneva. The first Presbyterian churches were established by John KNOX in 1560, when the Scottish parliament accepted a Calvinist confession of FAITH as the CREED of the realm. The term Presbyterian is based upon PRESBYTERS or councils of elders who administered the churches established by PAUL. The Presbyterian churches reject the episcopalian authority of BISHOPS and PRIESTS and elect a hierarchy of courts represented by MINISTERS and ELDERS. The courts function first at the local or KIRK level but the ultimate authority is the General Assembly. There are Presbyterian churches in Scotland, England, Hungary, France, Holland, Northern Ireland, Switzerland and the USA. (*See also* PRESBYTERY)

Presbytery The PRESBYTERIAN church court that has authority over a number of KIRKS or churches and is responsible for public worship and the appointment of MINISTERS. The term is also applied to the SANCTUARY. (*See also* PRESBYTER)

Priest The institution of CLERGY existing in the Episcopalian churches that derives its authority from the APOSTOLIC SUCCESSION from Jesus Christ (who is the culmination of Jewish priesthood in that his sacrifice reconciles humanity to God), down through the APOSTLES to an unbroken chain of BISHOPS. Priesthood in Christianity derives its authority from God and confers the supernatural function to consecrate the HOST, celebrate the EUCHARIST, provide ABSOLUTION of SIN in CONFESSION and minister all the remaining SACRAMENTS. The Protestant reformers were to reject the supernatural elements of the priesthood as unbiblical and to promote the ideal of a 'priesthood of all believers'. (*See also* CONSECRATION; MINISTER)

Prime Traditionally, the first divine OFFICE of the day held at 6 a.m. It was removed from the Roman Catholic Breviary in 1971 and combined with LAUDS. This pattern is generally followed by Anglican orders.

Primate The senior BISHOP who is the overall authority of a national Church or people. The POPE is the primate of the Roman Catholic Church, whereas the ARCHBISHOP of Canterbury is the primate of All England.

Prior / Prioress The title given to the head of a mendicant community, or a MONK/NUN who deputizes for the ABBOT/ABBESS and takes charge of a subsidiary or satellite house dependent on the abbey. (*See also* MENDICANT FRIARS; MONASTERY; ORDER)

Priory   The community under the authority of a PRIOR/PRIORESS.

Profession, Religious   The taking of the vows of chastity, poverty and OBEDIENCE that occurs at the end of a novitiate period and functions as the entry to full monastic life in a religious ORDER (*See also* MONK; NOVICE; NUN; RELIGIOUS).

Propitiation   *See* ATONEMENT.

Protestant   The term originated in the protest against the decision of the Diet of Speyer to end toleration of LUTHERANISM in Germany in 1529 and has become associated with the REFORMATION and all those Christians since then who have broken away from the beliefs and practices of the ROMAN CATHOLIC Church. The essential characteristics of Protestantism are the rejection of priesthood in favour of the 'priesthood of all believers', the acceptance of the BIBLE as the only source of revealed truth, and JUSTIFICATION by FAITH alone. The hearing of the word has also been given priority over sacramental practice. (*See also* CALVIN, JOHN; LUTHER, MARTIN; SACRAMENT; ZWINGLI, ULRICH)

Prothesis   A table or ALTAR in the Eastern ORTHODOX CHURCHES where the bread and wine to be used in the EUCHARIST are prepared. (*See also* LITURGY)

Psalms, Book of   The Jewish psalms have been used in Christian public and private devotions since very early times and certainly by the second century were regularly included in Christian LITURGY. They form an essential part of the regular divine OFFICES and are sung in morning and evening prayer. The book which contains the psalms and their place in the liturgical year is known as a psalter.

Psalter   *See* PSALMS.

Pulpit   A raised stand of stone or wood traditionally placed on the north side of the NAVE from which the PRIEST or preacher delivers the SERMON.

Purgatory   The Roman Catholic belief in a temporary place or state where believers who have died in a state of GRACE may receive the punishment for their VENIAL as opposed to MORTAL SINS. The pain of purgatory is relieved by the expectation of salvation and the granting of the BEATIFIC VISION to follow temporary punishment. Purgatory can also be relieved by the prayers of the faithful and the offering up of the REQUIEM MASS. (*See also* HELL)

Puritans   A pronounced form of English PROTESTANTISM associated with the DOCTRINES of CALVINISM, which attempted to reform the Elizabethan and Stuart Church of England by attacking church ornamentation and the institution of the EPISCOPACY. They were successful during the English revolution of 1642, but the term disappeared after the proliferation of NON-CONFORMIST sects at the Restoration of Charles II. However, the Puritan movement was transplanted to North America in the seventeenth century. (*See also* CALVIN, JOHN; PRESBYTERIAN)

Pyx   A small gold or silver box used by a PRIEST to carry the consecrated HOST when visiting the sick. (*See also* EUCHARIST)

Q

Q   The symbol given to the hypothetical text that is believed by some scholars to be a common source for passages in the GOSPELS of St MATTHEW and St LUKE which show remarkable similarity but differ from St MARK's Gospel. (*See also* SYNOPTIC GOSPELS)

Quakers   The Religious Society of Friends founded in the seventeenth century by George Fox. The central DOCTRINE is the presence of inner light or the direct working of Christ in the soul. It is this which leads to their rejection of the SACRAMENTS, the ministry and all set forms of worship. Quaker worship usually takes the form of the congregation sitting in silence unless any member is moved by the spirit to speak. Quakers are pacifist and renowned for their religious tolerance and involvement in charitable activities that espouse ecological or environmental issues.

Quinque Viae   The five arguments used by St Thomas AQUINAS to rationally demonstrate the existence of God. They are as follows:
1. The argument that everything that moves must be caused by something else. There must eventually be a prime mover from which all motion begins.
2. All effects must be traced back to a single cause.
3. The world contains contingent beings who are not essential. It is necessary is to explain why they exist. God is the necessary being that explains our existence.
4. There must be an origin to the human values of truth, goodness and nobility.

5. The world shows evidence of order and design which must be attributable to an intelligent creator.

Qumran   The site of the caves near the Dead Sea where the first of the DEAD SEA SCROLLS was found in 1947. (*See also* ESSENES)

Quo Vadis   *Lit. Where are you going?* According to a legend, this is the question asked by PETER when he met Christ on the road after fleeing for his life from Rome. Christ is believed to have replied that he was on his way to be crucified again. Peter returned to Rome where he became a MARTYR.

R

Ransom A term applied for the death of Jesus Christ which derived from the Greek custom of being able to buy the freedom of a slave. The term suggests that Jesus' death bought humanity its freedom from enslavement to SIN. (*See also* RECONCILIATION; REDEMPTION)

Ranters One of the Protestant sects of the seventeenth century who, like the QUAKERS, appealed to the inner experience of the individual as opposed to priesthood, Scripture and CREED.

Real Presence The belief in the actual presence of the body and blood of Christ in the bread and wine used in the EUCHARIST. (*See also* CONSUBSTANTIATION; TRANSUBSTANTIATION)

Receptionism A DOCTRINE concerning the EUCHARIST which states that the bread and wine are unchanged but the body and blood of Jesus enter the participant during the SACRAMENT. (*See also* CONSUBSTANTIATION; TRANSUBSTANTIATION)

Reconciliation There are four passages in the NEW TESTAMENT (Romans 5.10; 2 Corinthians 5.18; Ephesians 2.11 and Colossians 1.19) that perceive Jesus Christ as an offering or sacrifice to bridge the gap between sinful humankind and God. The theme of reconciliation is important, as it heals the enmity that has existed between human beings and their creator since the FALL of ADAM and EVE had left all humanity with the inheritance of ORIGINAL SIN. The reconciliation offered by the sacrifice of Jesus Christ was the new covenant or

REVELATION that made forgiveness of SIN possible. In the Roman Catholic Church, the SACRAMENT of CONFESSION is also known as reconciliation. (*See also* RANSOM)

Redaction criticism   The study of the Bible that seeks to explore the editorial processes which linked earlier and later texts. (*See also* FORM CRITICISM)

Redemption   The theological idea that God has freed human beings from SIN and death through INCARNATION as Jesus Christ. However, redemption goes beyond mere deliverance and is bound up with the idea of RANSOM or sacrifice. For example, in the Gospel of MARK (10.45) the writer speaks of Christ as being 'a ransom for many'. The Bible usually provides allegories for redemption that indicate a payment or price for deliverance. The death of Christ is regarded as the payment for the release of all human beings from the bondage of sin. (*See also* RECONCILIATION; REVELATION)

Reformation   The term used to describe a sixteenth-century Western European reform movement focused around individuals such as Martin LUTHER, Ulrich ZWINGLI and John CALVIN that led to the creation of the Protestant churches. It is traditionally believed to date from the protests of Luther against perceived corruptions in the Roman Catholic Church in 1517. However, earlier movements, such as the ANABAPTISTS, had called for a return to the simplicity and piety of the primitive Church. Although the reformers were concerned with the moral, theological and institutional reform of the Church, the actual agenda varied from country to country.

Reformed Churches   The Protestant churches that are historically associated with the doctrines of CALVIN and ZWINGLI as opposed to LUTHER. (*See also* CALVINISM, NON-CONFORMIST, PREDESTINATION; PRESBYTERIAN)

Regeneration   The theological idea that all creation is renewed through the INCARNATION of God in Jesus Christ. However, the individual participates fully in this through the transformation that takes place in accepting Jesus Christ. This transformation is seen as a new birth in which SIN is no longer in control. The HOLY SPIRIT guides the newly transformed human being. This spiritual rebirth is closely linked to BAPTISM and the NEW TESTAMENT writers suggest that the SACRAMENT is capable of initiating the transformative process. (*See also* REDEMPTION)

Regular   Members of the priesthood who are also bound by the vows of a religious ORDER and live in a religious community such as the BENEDICTINES or the JESUITS. (*See also* RELIGIOUS)

Relics   The venerated remains of SAINTS, or material objects which have been in contact with them, used as objects of devotion after their death. They are usually kept in a church, shrine or place of pilgrimage. (*See also* FERETORY; RELIQUARY)

Religious   A proper term for a member of a religious ORDER or monastic community such as a MONK, FRIAR or NUN. They may be categorized into active or contemplative communities; hermits or members of a community, mendicants or cloistered. Most religious are lay members of the church but it is possible for male religious to be PRIESTS. Recently, the nuns of the CHURCH OF ENGLAND have also been able to join the priesthood. (*See also* NOVICES; OBLATES; REGULAR)

Religious Society of Friends   *See* QUAKERS.

Reliquary   A container used for the RELICS of a SAINT. (*See also* FERETORY)

Repentance   The condemnation of SIN by the individual who has committed it, and the subsequent return to dependence on and obedience towards God. The NEW TESTAMENT suggests a state of remorse followed by transformation, or heartfelt change of behaviour, is required. In Christian theology, repentance and forgiveness are only possible because of the RECONCILIATION made possible through the sacrifice of Jesus Christ on the cross. In Christian practice, repentance usually consists of remorse, CONFESSION and an act of reparation which involves transformation. (*See also* RANSOM)

Reprobation   The belief maintained by some Christians, especially CALVINIST-influenced Protestants who believe in PREDESTINATION, that unrepentant sinners are condemned to eternal damnation. (*See also* REPENTANCE; SIN)

Requiem Mass   The service of the MASS or EUCHARIST offered for the dead which precedes the funeral. (*See also* SACRAMENT)

Reredos   Any kind of decoration placed above and behind the ALTAR in a church, such as murals, painted wooden panels or wall paintings. (*See also* SANCTUARY)

Resurrection   The FAITH in the resurrection or the rising from the dead attributed to Jesus Christ is central to Christian belief. The GOSPELS indicate the importance of the resurrection by the amount of coverage they give to the incidents leading up to Jesus' death. They clearly state that Jesus Christ was crucified, died, was placed in the tomb and then on the third day rose again from the dead. Over a period of time, Jesus then appeared to his DISCIPLES in the flesh. The resurrection not only restored the disciples to faith and provided the impetus for the spread of early Christianity; but it also formulated the Christian doctrine that Jesus had been finally victorious over death and confirmed his victory over SIN. Death had been the punishment for sin meted out to ADAM and EVE as a consequence of the FALL. The resurrection also contains the promise of resurrection for all believers with the PAROUSIA. The newly restored eternal life of Christ provides the possibility for a new life in Christ given by GRACE to a believing Christian. (*See also* CRUCIFIXION; RANSOM; RECONCILIATION; REDEMPTION)

Revelation   One of the central themes of Christian theology is the FAITH in the self-disclosure of God made throughout human history. The principle sources of the history of revelation are the OLD and NEW TESTAMENTS. It is generally agreed that human beings utilizing their own faculties are not able to comprehend the mystery of the divine and therefore require knowledge of God, which comes from what He has revealed and the process by which this takes place. Protestant

DENOMINATIONS generally believe that all revelation is contained in the BIBLE, whereas Roman Catholics believe that it is also contained in the unbroken tradition of the Church itself. (*See also* JESUS CHRIST)

Revelation, Book of   The last book of the NEW TESTAMENT, attributed to the APOSTLE JOHN, which consists of a series of apocalyptic visions concerning the end time. The book is written in an intensely symbolic style which is difficult for the modern reader to interpret. A major influence on Christian millennial movements, the book tells of the events that will take place when God finally intervenes in a catastrophic way to bring about His will. The book tells of the second coming of Christ, the final war with the forces of evil and the eventual triumph of God with the PAROUSIA. (*See also* MILLENNARI-ANISM)

Reverend   A title of respect applied to Christian CLERGY since the fifteenth century and used as the correct prefix in correspondence.

Revivalism   An EVANGELICAL type of worship based on public rallies, where great fervour is exhibited, often stimulated by preaching and prayer. The meetings are marked by the practice of calling up members of the audience either to testify to being touched by the HOLY SPIRIT or to affirm their renewal of Christian FAITH. (*See also* METHODISM)

Roman Catholic   That part of Christianity which gives its allegiance to the Bishop of Rome or the POPE, as opposed to the ORTHODOX CHURCH or PROTESTANT traditions. The Roman Catholic tradition presents itself as a hierarchical organization of BISHOPS and PRIESTS with the Pope at its head, in which the mysteries of the Church are mediated to the lay members through seven SACRAMENTS which can only be delivered through the priesthood. The centre of Roman Catholic worship is the LITURGY of the MASS and attendance is oblig-atory every Sunday. The Church also consists of several large monastic ORDERS and lay congregations which seek to combine contemplative life with the rigours of working in the world. (*See also* CARDINAL; SAINTS; VATICAN)

Romans, Epistle to the   The longest of the letters of PAUL which forms one of the books of the NEW TESTAMENT. It is written just before the APOSTLE completes his work in the eastern Mediterranean and turns his attention towards the West and his forthcoming visit to ROME. Paul provides his reasons for visiting Rome and outlines the reasons why God rejected Israel and brought salvation to the GENTILES. As a Roman citizen, Paul was aware of the importance of the young Church at the heart of the Roman Empire and this influenced his reasons for writing the EPISTLE.

Rome   By the time of Paul's ministry, there is already a fledgling Christian community in the heart of the Roman Empire. Paul passed two years in Rome and by the second century of Christian history, a tradition had developed that Peter had worked in Rome and become a MARTYR there. Certainly by the time of Nero, Roman accounts indicate that there were many Christians in the city, and it later became the centre of the Christian Church until CONSTANTINE moved his capital to Constantinople in 330. In the seventh century, relationships between the Church in the East and the Church in Rome deteriorated and eventually they divided, leaving Rome as the centre of Western Christianity and the capital of the Holy Roman Empire until the founding of the Protestant churches. (*See also* ROMAN CATHOLIC; ROMANS, EPISTLE TO)

Rosary   The most common method of popular devotion, in which prayers are counted on beads in order to assist the memory. The most important prayer associated with the rosary is the devotion to the fifteen mysteries arranged in groups of five which articulate the essential events in the life of Jesus Christ and his mother MARY. Each item in the rosary is formed of one LORD'S PRAYER, which precedes ten 'Hail Marys' followed by the Gloria Patri. Every five decades of Hail Marys, known as a chaplet, is preceded by the APOSTLES' CREED. (*See also* CONFESSION)

Rural Dean   The title for a PRIEST in the CHURCH OF ENGLAND who is in charge of a group of PARISHES and appointed by the BISHOP of the DIOCESE.

S

Sabbatarianism Certain Christian movements that observe the Sabbath very strictly and argue that the SABBATH laws should be followed on the basis of OLD TESTAMENT restrictions, or alternatively advocate strict observance of the Sabbath nationally. Particularly strong in Britain's puritan traditions, this influence has been growing progressively weaker since the nineteenth century.

Sabbath The early Church maintained the Jewish Sabbath, which celebrates the seventh day when God rested from the act of creation. However, as Christianity spread to the GENTILE world, this was changed to Sunday to coincide with the day of Jesus Christ's RESURRECTION from the dead. Christians use it as a day of worship and religious education for children. There are some Christians, however, who maintain that no work should be done on the Sabbath unless it is an act of goodness or charity. (*See also* SABBATARIANISM; SUNDAY SCHOOL)

Sacrament Certain rites of the Church which are defined as an outward, visible sign ordained by Christ of an inward spiritual blessing. Thus for the Roman Catholic Church, the seven SACRAMENTS of BAPTISM, CONFIRMATION, Matrimony, ORDERS, EUCHARIST, PENANCE, and UNCTION are the main ways in which the presence of God manifests itself in the Church. However, the Protestant churches argue that the NEW TESTAMENT only refers to two sacraments: baptism and the Eucharist.

Sacramentals   Certain religious practices which, according to Roman Catholicism, are similar to the seven SACRAMENTS but not as important, as they do not carry the GRACE of God. However, they help to make daily life sacred and carry spiritual effects. They include the sign of the cross and saying of grace at meals.

Sacred College   *See* COLLEGE.

Sacred Heart   Devotion to the physical heart of Jesus, often followed by mystics, that originated in the medieval period. In the Roman Catholic Church, such devotion is observed on the Friday after Corpus Christi, the feast that commemorates the institution of the EUCHARIST on the Thursday after Trinity Sunday.

Sacristan   An alternative title for a SEXTON or an official who has responsibility for the contents of the SACRISTY, namely the VESTMENTS and the vessels used in the EUCHARIST.

Sacristy   A room for keeping the vessels used in the EUCHARIST and used as a changing room by the CLERGY. (*See also* SACRISTAN; VESTRY)

Sadducees   A Jewish sect at the time of Jesus who were opposed to the PHARISEES. They were influential in JERUSALEM and at the Temple, where many of them were members of the SANHEDRIN. The GOSPELS present them as opposing Jesus and his DISCIPLES very vigorously and they are depicted as proud, arrogant and rigid in their application of Jewish law.

Saint   The term used in early Christianity to denote people who were set apart as hallowed or consecrated to God. It is derived from the Latin *sanctus*, which in turn is a translation of the Greek *hagios*. It was first used in a Christian context by St PAUL when he addressed the Christian communities as saints. Paul was referring to every member of the community being sacred or consecrated to God as the new ISRAEL called to sanctity and God's service. Later the term was applied individually to the MARTYRS, those that died in God's service. Gradually, the term 'saint' was applied to special individuals such as BISHOPS or

MONKS. From this developed its present-day usage as a title of honour conferred on an individual who has lived a life of devotion to Christ to a degree that marks them out amongst their fellow Christians. The Roman Catholic Church employs an official process known as CANONIZATION, in which the individual is investigated and awarded sainthood by the POPE. (*See also* APOSTLES; BEATIFICATION; SAINTS, DEVOTION TO)

Saint Paul's Cathedral   A church in London originally built in 607. It was burned down in 1666 in the Fire of London and rebuilt by Sir Christopher Wren. It is often used for official and some state occasions.

Saint Peter's, Rome   The original church is believed to have been built on the site of PETER's crucifixion in ROME, but the present building dates from the sixteenth century. It is the apostle's traditional burial place and the public face of the Vatican. It stands at the end of St Peter's Square in Rome where the POPE traditionally blesses the faithful from a balcony. (*See also* VATICAN)

Saints, Devotion to   The practice of venerating and calling upon SAINTS for intercession which remains a strong element of Roman Catholic worship. During the first thousand years of Christian history, veneration of departed Christians was mainly reserved for MARTYRS but the medieval period saw a marked increase in the belief in and demand for miracles, which was centred in a cult of saints. Devotees began to pray to saints to intervene miraculously in their own lives, and miracles became the proof of sainthood. The veneration of saint's RELICS became increasingly popular and they were placed on church altars as well as in their own shrines and basilicas. As the number of saints proliferated, so did saints' feast days and the assigning of special roles to particular individuals. (*See also* ALL SAINTS' DAY; FERETORY; PATRON SAINT, RELIQUARY)

Salvation   *See* REDEMPTION.

Salvation Army / Salvationist   An international Protestant Christian organization for evangelical work founded by William Booth in

1865. Its individual members are sometimes referred to as Salvationists. Organized on a military basis, it is well known for its uniformed evangelists who play in brass bands and participate in social work amongst the poor and needy. They are unusual amongst Christian movements in that they do not accept any SACRAMENTS.

Sanctification   The process by which a believer is made holy by following the teachings and actions of Jesus Christ or participating in the SACRAMENTS. It refers to an inward process that takes place gradually and effects a change of character leading to an outward life of virtue and godliness. PAUL talks of sanctification as the gift of new life made possible by FAITH in Jesus Christ. (*See also* JUSTIFICATION; REDEMPTION)

Sanctuary   In the OLD TESTAMENT it refers to a place set apart for the worship of God. The highest Jewish sanctuary was the Temple in JERUSALEM. In Christianity, the term applies to the most sacred part of a church, which contains the ALTAR and the choir stalls and lies beyond the NAVE at the eastern end of the church.

Sanhedrin   The supreme court and council of the Jews that met in JERUSALEM. Several of the early Christians found themselves on trial by the Sanhedrin including PETER, JOHN and PAUL. The council was also involved in the decision to stone STEPHEN to death. However, they are most remembered in Christianity as presiding over the trial of Jesus Christ and pronouncing his death sentence for the charge of blasphemy. (*See also* CRUCIFIXION)

Santa Sophia   One of the most famous churches in Eastern Christianity built in Constantinople by the Emperor Justinian in 538 CE. In 1453 it was converted into a mosque but is now a museum in the city of Istanbul. However, both Christians and Muslims are allowed to pray in separated parts of the building.

Satan   Also known as the Devil. The leader of the spirits and chief of the devils who are opposed to God. He is traditionally believed to be a fallen angel. In the OLD TESTAMENT, Satan occasionally appears as a figure who is always perverted, corrupting or working against the best interests of human beings. However, in the NEW TESTAMENT, he is identified with the personification of evil and is always hostile to God and his purposes. The GOSPEL writers MATTHEW and LUKE recount that Satan tempted Jesus Christ during his 40-day retreat at the commencement of his ministry. The New Testament presents the history of humanity as a war between the forces of good, loyal to God, and the forces of evil led by Satan. The final overthrow of Satan's dominion on earth began with Christ's death and resurrection and will be completed at the second coming of Jesus Christ. (*See also* LUCIFER; PAROUSIA; TEMPTATION)

Satisfaction   A theological doctrine linked to Anselm of Canterbury (d. 1109). It proposes that the death of Christ was offered to God as an ATONEMENT to make amends for the affront of human SIN. Anselm argued that God had originally meant human beings to be righteous creations capable of eternal life. However, such a state is dependent on obedience. Human disobedience led to a state of sin, which had to be atoned for in order to restore human beings to righteousness. As human beings were not themselves capable of providing the satisfaction, or atonement price, a 'God-man' was necessary. The INCARNATION of Jesus Christ provides both the ability and the will to pay the atonement price. (*See also* CRUCIFIXION; REDEMPTION; RESURRECTION)

Scholasticism   A particular approach to Christian theology associated with the medieval period in which the use of the intellect is advocated to understand revealed truth through philosophical or theological speculation. Scholasticism is not a movement but a system of organizing knowledge by making fine distinctions. The most influential user of scholasticism to provide a body of theology was Thomas AQUINAS.

Second Adam   A title for Jesus Christ used by PAUL which refers to Christ's role as the leader of redeemed humanity, as opposed to ADAM, who was responsible for the FALL (*See also* ATONEMENT; REDEMPTION; SIN).

Second Coming *See* PAROUSIA.

See The official throne of a BISHOP which is normally kept in a CATHEDRAL and which denotes the bishop's authority over a DIOCESE. (*See also* ENTHRONIZATION; HOLY SEE)

Seminary Theological colleges for the training of the priesthood maintained by both the Roman Catholic and Anglican churches. (*See also* PRIEST)

Septuagesima The third Sunday before LENT and the seventh before EASTER celebrated in the CHURCH OF ENGLAND's liturgical year.

Sermon Used in a general sense to describe a (possibly published) discourse on a religious or moral subject. In the specific sense, the sermon is delivered from the PULPIT and used for instruction or exhortation of the congregation. The theme of the sermon is taken from the LESSON, the scriptural passages from the GOSPELS and the EPISTLES read according to the liturgical year.

Sermon on the Mount The famous discourse of Jesus described in Chapter 5 of MATTHEW's GOSPEL which provides the basis of Christian ethics. (*See also* BEATITUDES; LORD'S PRAYER)

Server One who assists the PRIEST at the EUCHARIST by making the responses, washing the hands of the celebrant and bringing the HOST to the altar.

Seven Churches The seven early communities of Christians in Asia Minor which are addressed in the Book of REVELATION in the NEW TESTAMENT. They are Ephesus, Smyrna, Pergamum, Thyatira, Sardis, Philadelphia and Laodicea.

Seven Deadly Sins The seven SINS of pride, anger, lust, envy, gluttony, sloth and covetousness that can damn the human soul to an eternity of separation from the presence of God.

Seven Sacraments   *See* SACRAMENT.

Seven Virtues   The qualities of FAITH, HOPE, LOVE, fortitude, temperance, justice and prudence, whose cultivation is considered to be the ideal for human life. (*See also* SEVEN DEADLY SINS)

Seventh Day Adventists   A group of Protestant ADVENTISTS who formed in 1863 and who observe adult BAPTISM, temperance and maintain the SABBATH from sunset on Friday until sunset on Saturday.

Sexagesima   The second Sunday before LENT and the sixth before EASTER celebrated in the CHURCH OF ENGLAND's liturgical year.

Sign of the Cross   An important Christian blessing made by bringing the right hand from the forehead to the breast and then from shoulder to shoulder. It is used to sanctify and bless various occasions and as a sign of recognition during periods of persecution.

Simon Peter   *See* PETER, ST.

Sin   Sin, sometimes referred to as formal sin, is an intentional act of rebellion or disobedience against the known will of God and a falling away from the moral condition of righteousness in which the human race was created. Death, punishment in HELL and the denial of God's presence are the penalties of sin. The state of sin is the human condition and ruling principle of human life since the FALL of ADAM and EVE and consequently human beings are in need of transformation or regeneration which becomes possible through the death and RESURRECTION of Jesus Christ. (*See also* ATONEMENT; HEAVEN; REDEMPTION; SATAN; SATISFACTION)

Sisters of Mercy   A name commonly used for a member of a RELIGIOUS community engaged in nursing or other social activities on behalf of the poor and the sick. (*See also* MENDICANT FRIARS; NUNS)

Society of Friends   *See* QUAKERS.

Solifidianism   The doctrine of JUSTIFICATION by FAITH alone asserted by the Protestant reformers.

Son of God   The title given to Christ denoting the majesty of his divinity and referring to his role as the second aspect of the TRINITY. It points to the belief that God incarnated in human form as Jesus Christ, which is fully explored in the LOGOS principle described in JOHN's GOSPEL. (*See also* INCARNATION; SON OF MAN)

Son of Man   A title which Jesus Christ gave to himself. It is difficult to ascertain the origins of the term but traditionally it is used to describe Christ's humanity and the HUMILITY of the INCARNATION. It is also used to denote the universal nature of Christ's mission. (*See also* SON OF GOD)

Soteriology   The branch of theology that deals with salvation. In Christianity it is concerned with the FALL of humankind and SIN, GRACE and eternal life, the redemptive role of God in human history and the ATONEMENT in Christ. (*See also* PAROUSIA; REDEMPTION; RESURRECTION)

Spirit   *See* HOLY SPIRIT.

Stations of the Cross   A series of 14 places on the Via Dolorosa in JERUSALEM which is supposed to be the route that Jesus Christ took on his way from trial to CRUCIFIXION. The series presents the various episodes in the death of Christ based on biblical and non-biblical sources and it remains a popular form of devotion for pilgrims to visit and meditate upon each station. From the Middle Ages, pilgrims who could not afford to visit the Holy Land adopted the custom of circum-ambulating their parish churches, where depictions of the stations of the cross would be displayed as statues in stained-glass windows.

Stephen, St   One of the seven men appointed by the APOSTLES as the first DEACONS with the duty of looking after the distribution of alms to the poor and deprived in the early Christian communities. He was also a fervent missionary and preacher of the GOSPEL. As a Hellenistic Jew, he was brought before the SANHEDRIN on the charge of blasphemy. He boldly denounced the Council as the murderers of the MESSIAH and announced that he saw Jesus at the right hand of God. He was sentenced to death by stoning and thus became the first Christian MARTYR. Stephen is important because his death speech was the first clear articulation of the universal application of the Christian message, and his death was probably one of the factors in the conversion of PAUL who was present at the stoning.

Stigmata   The apparent miraculous manifestation of the wounds of Jesus Christ in the hands and feet of a worshipper either as invisible sites of pain or visible areas of bleeding. Stigmata can also appear around the head, where the crown of thorns was placed on Christ, or on the back and shoulders, where he was scourged. The first stigmatization in Christianity is attributed to St FRANCIS OF ASSISI.

Submersion   This type of BAPTISM involves completely covering the body in water, and is usually associated with adult baptism. Some Protestant DENOMINATIONS insist upon a baptism in which the believer enters a pool and is completely submerged. (*See also* ANABAPTISTS; BAPTISTS; BELIEVER'S BAPTISM)

Subordinationism   An early Christological argument that existed in the first three centuries of Christian history and asserts that the Son is under the Father and the HOLY SPIRIT is under the dominion of the Father and the Son. (*See also* ARIANISM; CHRISTOLOGY; FILOQUE; NICAEA, COUNCIL OF; TRINITARIAN; TRINITY)

Summa Theologica   The principal theological work of Thomas AQUINAS (1225–74). It is divided into three parts which deal with, respectively, God the creator, the restoration of humanity to God and, finally, the means by which the individual can bring about the salvation of humanity through joining the work of Christ. The work develops a systematic theology of the relationship between FAITH and reason and arguments for the divinity of Christ. (*See also* SCHOLASTICISM)

Sunday   *See* SABBATH.

Sunday Schools   Schools for providing religious instruction to children founded in 1780 by Robert Raikes (1735–1811). Originally, the schools provided both religious instruction and education in reading, writing and arithmetic with paid teachers. But as full-time public education was introduced, the secular curriculum disappeared and the teachers became voluntary members drawn from the local PARISH. Sunday schools continue to educate children into the fundamentals of Christian life in Britain and they are organized on a parish basis.

Superior   The title frequently used for the head of a RELIGIOUS ORDER – for example, Mother Superior (*See also* ABBESS; ABBOT; GENERAL).

Surplice   A loose white garment with wide sleeves that is placed over a CASSOCK and worn by both CLERGY and some lay participants, such as choir members and servers, and used in liturgical worship.

Synod   *See* COUNCIL.

Synoptic Gospels   A term applied to the GOSPELS of MATTHEW, MARK and LUKE and their presentation of the life of Jesus as contrasted with that in the Gospel of JOHN. Synoptic means having a common viewpoint, and arguments have taken place amongst scholars as to whether Mark or Matthew was the first gospel. Others argue that there was a common original oral or written source for the Synoptic Gospels. (*See also* LUKE, GOSPEL OF; MARK, GOSPEL OF; MATTHEW, GOSPEL OF; NEW TESTAMENT)

T

Tabernacle   A container for the vessels and the consecrated elements of bread and wine usually kept on the ALTAR in a side CHAPEL and marked by a lit candle. Normally only used by Roman Catholic and Eastern churches. (*See also* CONSECRATION; EUCHARIST)

Taize   An ecumenical monastic community founded in southern France in 1940 and famous for its work in promoting Christian unity and attracting young Christians. The MONKS wear ordinary clothing and only perform three offices a day instead of the customary seven. (*See also* OFFICES, DIVINE)

Temperance   The control of passion and sense pleasure which is regarded as one of the four cardinal virtues in Christianity. The need for self-control is associated with the Christian belief that the body is the temple of the HOLY SPIRIT. In the nineteenth century, a number of Christian organizations, especially associated with METHODISM, sprang up to counter the abuse of alcohol amongst the British working classes. These were known as Temperance Societies.

Templars   A military order also known as the Knights Templars or Knights of the Temple founded by Hugo de Payens in 1119 and so named because it was bequeathed land near the site of the old Jewish Temple in JERUSALEM. Bernard de Clairvaux (1090–1153) created a rule for them based on the CISTERCIANS and they were popular throughout Western Christianity. Their remit was to protect the pilgrims en route to the Holy Land, to defend the Holy Land and to fight with infidels. During the twelfth and thirteenth centuries they had considerable influence in Europe as a result of the CRUSADES and they became the greatest landowners in Europe. The end of the Crusades brought about their suppression and eventual destruction in the early fourteenth century. (*See also* HOSPITALLERS)

Temptation   The incitement to SIN which is the consequence of free will but also carries connotations of testing or trial by God with the benevolent intention of improving character or godly qualities. In the NEW TESTAMENT, trials or temptations can be either the work of God or SATAN. Although temptations form part of God's will, the desire to fall prey to sin belongs to the human being. Temptation in itself is not sin, and only becomes so when the human being gives in and performs the particular sinful act. (*See also* ATONEMENT; ORIGINAL SIN; TEMPTATION OF CHRIST)

Temptation of Christ   The unsuccessful attempt by SATAN to corrupt Christ after his 40-day vigil in the desert described in two of the Gospels (Matthew 4.1; Luke 22.28). The temptations were essentially concerned with Christ using the spiritual power given to him for worldly ambitions and temporal power. Christ, although tempted, remained sinless and provided the example for his DISCIPLES to resist TEMPTATION.

Teresa of Avila, St   (1515–82). A Spanish CARMELITE NUN and well-known mystic who, along with her disciple, St John of the Cross (1542–91), provided the example of a life of pious, self-renouncing contemplation expressed through silent PRAYER that resulted in ecstatic inner union with God. Together they reformed the Carmelite ORDER in Spain and provided a monastic model that united active and contemplative orders. She is famous for her efforts to provide a methodology to the mystical path by describing the various states that exist between discursive meditation and ecstasy. These can be found in her two books, *The Way of Perfection* and *The Interior Castle*.

Tertiary   The 'third order' or Order of Penitence first created by the FRANCISCANS in the twelfth century and extended to all the mendicant

ORDERS. It allowed membership of certain RELIGIOUS communities but does not involve withdrawal from the world. Both men and women can be employed in normal occupations and live a semi-monastic life of prayer, fasting, pacifism and worship. (*See also* DOMINICANS; MENDICANT FRIARS)

Theotokos   *Lit. the God-bearer.* A title given to MARY, the Mother of Jesus.

Thessalonians, Epistles to the   Two NEW TESTAMENTS books which were originally written as letters by St PAUL to the church in Thessalonica. They are important documents in that they provide insights into the Christian faith only 20 years after Jesus Christ's death. Paul had been in Thessalonica preaching in 50 CE but had left to avoid persecution after making a number of converts. TIMOTHY had been sent back to confirm the converts in their new faith by further teaching. He had reported back to Paul the strength of the fledgling church but indicated problems with ethical teachings concerning sexuality and eschatological concerns regarding the status of dead Christians at the PAROUSIA. The letters were written to answer their concerns and express Paul's joy at their maintenance of the faith. (*See also* EPISTLES)

Thirty-nine Articles   Short summaries or Protestant dogmatic tenets used by the CHURCH OF ENGLAND to formulate its doctrinal position. They were first published in 1563, but received their final form in 1571. Since 1875, newly ordained CLERGY are required to affirm the doctrines formally by giving a general assent to the beliefs enshrined in the Thirty-Nine Articles, but in practice little attempt is made to enforce them.

Thomas, St   One of the original twelve APOSTLES who were chosen by Jesus Christ as his companions and missionaries. He appears in the GOSPEL of St JOHN on several occasions but he is famous for doubting the RESURRECTION of Jesus Christ by asking to feel the wounds inflicted by the CRUCIFIXION after missing the occasion of the first appearance of Jesus to his DISCIPLES. This has given rise to the saying 'Doubting Thomas'. Some traditions believe that he spread

Christianity to Persia and India, and some forms of Christianity in South India call themselves the MAR THOMA Church as they believe it was founded by Thomas.

Thomas Aquinas, St   *See* AQUINAS, ST THOMAS.

Thomism   The systemised philosophical and theological study of the doctrines of Thomas Aquinas. (*See also* SCHOLASTICISM; AQUINAS, THOMAS)

Thurible   A container with chains used for the ritual burning of incense. It is swung back and forth by the Thurifer in Roman Catholic processions, ceremonies and services.

Thurifer   *See* THURIBLE.

Timothy, St   A friend and companion of St PAUL who may have been converted by him on his first missionary journey and who accompanied the APOSTLE on his second missionary journey. Timothy was entrusted with several important lone missions, including to Thessalonica, where he was able to encourage the persecuted Christians, and then to Corinth. He accompanied Paul to Corinth, Ephesus and JERUSALEM. He is last mentioned in Ephesus, where he was entrusted with the tasks of combating false teachers and the supervision of public worship. (*See also* THESSALONIANS, EPISTLES TO THE; TIMOTHY AND TITUS, STS, EPISTLES TO)

Timothy and Titus, Sts, Epistles to   Three NEW TESTAMENT books believed to have been written as pastoral letters by PAUL, of which two are addressed to TIMOTHY and one to TITUS. There have been some disputes concerning their authorship. While the content of the letters deals with the ecclesiastical organization of the early Church, they were probably written by the APOSTLE to encourage and teach two of his closest and most trusted companions, whom he probably perceived as the next generation to continue his missionary activities. (*See also* EPISTLES)

Tithes   The practice of supporting the CLERGY and the Church from the offerings of the laity, biblically based on OLD TESTAMENT customs in which a tenth of all produce was given to God by offering it to the Levites, who fulfilled the priestly office. The NEW TESTAMENT makes only two references to tithing but it became the traditional practice of the church and the payment remained one-tenth of all produce or income. Modern church practice has almost completely abolished tithing, although there are some Christians who argue that it is based on scriptural authority and should therefore be maintained.

Titus, St   A trusted companion of St PAUL and an early church missionary who accompanied PAUL and BARNABUS to JERUSALEM at the time of the GENTILE controversy. He acted as a reconciliator between Paul and the church in Corinth. He was in Crete with Paul and later church tradition describes how, in advanced old age, he was the BISHOP of the island. (*See also* TIMOTHY AND TITUS, STS, EPISTLES TO)

Tonsure   The distinctive style of shaving the centre of the head traditionally associated with MONKS and FRIARS. Most ORDERS now follow their own customs according to choice.

Tractarianism   The name given to the early development of the OXFORD MOVEMENT, so called because of their successful use of tracts, or leaflets. From 1832, John Henry Newman (1801–90) began publishing his famous *Tracts for the Times*. Overall, 90 tracts were published by Newman and the other leaders of the Oxford Movement, Richard Froude (1803–36), John Keble (1792–1866) and Edward Pusey (1800–82). Increasingly the *Tracts* reflected DOCTRINES and practices that were identified as primitive Christianity but were also popularly associated with Roman Catholicism. (*See also* HIGH CHURCH)

Tradition   In the early Church, tradition was used to describe the continuous REVELATION from God to His people through a succession of prophets and APOSTLES. The challenge of GNOSTICISM led the early generations of Christian leaders to define tradition as the act of handing down a carefully preserved expression of the teachings contained in the canon of Scripture, which ensures that the teachings of the Church in any one generation or period of time is the same GOSPEL proclaimed from the time of the apostles. Thus 'tradition' now refers to the accumulated wisdom and experience of the Church throughout its history. The Roman Catholic position has always been that tradition and Scripture have equal authority, whereas Protestants focus on Scripture alone. (*See also* APOSTOLIC SUCCESSION)

Transfiguration   The term used to describe the event recorded by the SYNOPTIC GOSPEL writers in which Jesus Christ appears as the Lord in full glory accompanied by the Jewish prophets Moses and Elijah, and witnessed by his three closest DISCIPLES PETER, JOHN and JAMES (Matthew 17.1–8; Mark 9.2–8; Luke 9.28–36). They accompanied Jesus up to the summit of a mountain, where they witnessed his transformation; the GOSPELS record that a voice spoke from a cloud declaring that Christ's Sonship and divine authority. The transfiguration functions to affirm Christ's divinity and demonstrates how he fulfils the REVELATION made earlier by God through the Jewish prophets. It also looks forward to the RESURRECTION and ASCENSION.

Transubstantiation   The traditional DOCTRINE associated with the Roman Catholic position that asserts that the elements of bread and wine used in the EUCHARIST are transformed into the body and blood of Jesus Christ at the time of CONSECRATION. The doctrine rests upon Thomas AQUINAS' interpretation of Aristotle's distinction between accident and substance: the substance of a thing is its real nature whereas its accidents are its outward appearances. Therefore the doctrine of transubstantiation is able to posit that while the accidents of bread and wine remain the same, their substances are transformed by the Eucharistic rite. (*See also* CONSUBSTANTIATION)

Trappists   A reform movement of the CISTERCIAN RELIGIOUS ORDER founded in 1662 and properly known as the Cistercians of the Strict Observance. It is renowned for its austerity and silence.

Trent, Council of   (1545–63) A Council called by the Roman Catholic Church to counter the REFORMATION and develop a theological response to the challenge of Martin LUTHER. It also attempted to reestablish the Church through a renewal of spiritual discipline and moral life. The reforming process became known as the Counter-Reformation. The Church clarified and reformed its position on JUSTIFICATION, SACRAMENTS, relationship between scripture and TRADITION and reviewed the behaviour of CLERGY, ecclesiastical discipline, religious education and missionary activity.

Trinitarian   The doctrine of the TRINITY or a person who believes in that DOCTRINE. The Trinitarian position is one of the main markers of Christian ORTHODOXY, although there are differences of doctrine between the Western and Eastern churches. The basis of the doctrine rests in the belief that the three aspects of the Trinity are to be regarded as possessing equal divinity and equal status. The co-equality of the Father and the Son was established at the Council of NICAEA. The Eastern churches have focused attention on the relationship by considering how the three aspects may be experienced in the life of a Christian. The Western position is more theological. (*See also* BINITARIANISM; UNITARIANISM)

Trinity   The doctrine maintained by all mainstream forms of Christianity in which there are three persons within the Godhead – Father, Son and the HOLY SPIRIT. All three are equally divine and have the same status. Two distinctive positions were to develop in regard to understanding the Trinity. The Eastern Church focused on considering the different ways in which the Father, Son and Holy Spirit were experienced, emphasizing the function of each independent aspect of the Godhead. The Western Church focused on the unity of the Godhead and perceived the Trinity as relational. The doctrine originally arose out of early Christian debate concerning the divinity of Jesus Christ. This growing belief in Christ's divinity necessitated understanding his relationship to the creator God. At a later date the concept of unity was extended to include the Holy Spirit. (*See also* CHRISTOLOGY; FILIOQUE; HOMOIOUSIOS; NICEA, COUNCIL OF; TRINITARIAN; UNITARIANISM)

Trinity Sunday   One of the holy days marked out in the Christian liturgical calendar. It marks the transition between the first six months, known as the half-year of Christ, and the second six months, known as the half-year of the Church. It is celebrated on the first Sunday after PENTECOST or WHITSUN and is dedicated to the TRINITY. (*See also* TRINITARIAN)

U

Unction   One of the seven SACRAMENTS observed by Roman Catholics and the ORTHODOX CHURCH in which a sick or dying person is anointed with oil by a PRIEST. The Roman Catholics generally perform the sacrament when it is believed that there is no hope of recovery but in Eastern Orthodoxy it is used for healing. Anointing with oil is also used in Britain to anoint the monarch at a coronation ceremony.

Unitarianism   A type of Christian thought and religious practice that rejects the DOCTRINE of the TRINITY and the divinity of Jesus Christ. The first organized communities appeared in the sixteenth century in Poland, Hungary and England. The first Unitarian DENOMINATION was founded in Britain in 1773 as a breakaway from the CHURCH OF ENGLAND. In the USA, Unitarianism dates back to the late eighteenth century. Contemporary Unitarianism is divided between those who follow traditional non-conformist Protestant Christianity but reject Trinitarianism as non-biblical, and those who espouse a pluralist position drawing upon inspiration from many of the world's religious and spiritual figures. (*See also* REFORMATION; TRINITARIAN)

United Reformed Church   A Protestant DENOMINATION formed in Britain by the union of CONGREGATIONALISTS and English PRESBYTERIANS in 1972.

Universalism   The theological position that all people will eventually achieve salvation regardless of whether they have accepted the Christian proclamation of REDEMPTION through Jesus Christ. This position arises from the belief that a God of Love could not allow evil to triumph. The earliest exponent was ORIGEN, one of the early Church fathers.

V

Valentine, St St Valentine's Day (14 February) was originally associated with a Christian MARTYR of that name. The association with romantic love probably derives from a seasonal pagan festival also held in February.

Vatican A self-governing state situated in the city of ROME which functions as the residence of the POPE and the administrative centre of the Roman Catholic Church.

Vatican Council I (1869–70) An important council, as it tackled the question of the POPE's authority and declared INFALLIBILITY to be a tenet of the Catholic faith. It clearly maintained the principle of infallibility but only on the occasions when the Pope is defining DOCTRINE on a matter of FAITH or morality. However, it was considered a defeat by church liberals who wanted to maintain authority in the Council of Bishops.

Vatican Council II (1962–5) The famous reforming council held by Pope John XXIII, and otherwise known as the Twenty-first Ecumenical Council, was called to modernize the teachings, discipline, liturgy and organization of the Church with a view to the eventual unity of all DENOMINATIONS, or, at least, closer cooperation with the ecumenical movement. The main changes were the use of the vernacular instead of Latin in the EUCHARIST, greater participation of the laity, an acknowledgement of modern biblical scholarship and increased participation in ECUMENISM.

134

Venerable   The title given to someone in the Roman Catholic Church after BEATIFICATION. It is also the official title given to an ARCHDEACON in the CHURCH OF ENGLAND.

Venial Sin   In Roman Catholic DOCTRINE it describes a sinful act which does not remove the sinner from the receipt of the GRACE of God or lead to eternal damnation like a MORTAL sin. However, it can still result in a period of PURGATORY unless confessed and forgiven. (*See also* SIN)

Verger   The lay official who takes care of the interior of a church.

Vespers   The evening prayer office celebrated along with MATINS (morning prayer) from the first centuries of Christianity. The daily offices were maintained in the cathedrals and monasteries in the Middle Ages but the Lutheran REFORMATION brought them back as daily congregational worship. The evening office usually consists of a minimum of two or three PSALMS, the ANTIPHON, LESSON, MAGNIFICAT, COLLECT, LITANY and BENEDICAMUS. (*See also* OFFICE, DIVINE)

Vestments   The distinctive historic dress consisting of a knee-length SURPLICE, full-length CASSOCK and stole worn by the CLERGY when participating in worship. Roman Catholics and Anglo-Catholics vary the colours of the vestments based upon the liturgical year. NONCONFORMIST Protestants traditionally only wear a cassock and gown in black and white throughout the year. Some Protestant movements may not wear vestments as they associate them with priesthood. (*See also* COPE)

Vestry   A room in a church where the VESTMENTS and ritual objects required in public worship are kept when not in use. The CLERGY use it as a dressing room before and after worship. (*See also* EUCHARIST; VESTMENTS)

Via Dolorosa   The road through JERUSALEM that Christ is believed to have taken on his way to CRUCIFIXION after leaving the judgement hall of PONTIUS PILATE. It is a major place of pilgrimage for Christians, as it contains the fourteen STATIONS OF THE CROSS, or sites of major incidents that took place on the route to crucifixion. Pilgrims will recite prayers and meditate on each incident.

Viaticum   *Lit. provision for a journey.* The final Communion given to those considered about to die in order to provide the spiritual sustenance for the journey to the afterlife. (*See also* EUCHARIST; UNCTION)

Vicar   The title given to a PARISH PRIEST in the CHURCH OF ENGLAND. The title 'the Vicar of Christ' is also given to the POPE.

Vicar of Christ   *See* POPE.

Vigil   Periods of prayer that go on through the night and usually end with the EUCHARIST in the morning. Although common in the early Church, they were abolished in the 1969 calendar of the Roman Catholic Church. The only remaining vigil in the Christian calendar takes place at EASTER, traditionally on MAUNDY THURSDAY, the night before GOOD FRIDAY, and commemorates the vigil in the Garden of GETHSEMANE, where Jesus and his DISCIPLES spent the night before his arrest.

Virgin Birth   The DOCTRINE that states that Christ was miraculously conceived of the Virgin MARY through the power of the HOLY SPIRIT and without a human father. While Protestants believe only in a virginal conception, Roman Catholics believe that the birth itself was a miraculous event which left Mary intact. This supports the Catholic DOCTRINE that insists that Mary remained a virgin throughout her life. The virgin birth is based upon the GOSPEL accounts of MATTHEW and LUKE. Since the second half of the twentieth century it has come under increasing attack from liberal theologians but still remains ORTHODOX Christian doctrine.

Virgin Mary   *See* MARY, THE BLESSED VIRGIN.

Virtualism   One of the several DOCTRINES formulated to explain the relationship between the eucharistic bread and wine and the body and blood of Christ. The doctrine of virtualism states that the bread and wine are not changed into the body and blood of Jesus Christ by act of CONSECRATION but that the faithful participating in the rite receive the body and blood of Christ through the agency of the bread and wine. (*See also* CONSUBSTANTIATION; HOST; TRANSUBSTANTIATION)

Visitation of the Sick   The duty of a PRIEST to ensure that PRAYERS, blessing, confession and MASS are available to those not able to attend public worship through ill health. (*See also* UNCTION; VIATICUM)

Voluntarism   The theological position posited by William of Ockham, a medieval theologian, which states that God was not under any obligation to reward good deeds. He argued that the position contended by Thomas AQUINAS, in which God recognized the value of an action, limited the freedom of the divine will.

Vulgate   The Latin version of the Bible translated by St Jerome from 382 onwards. When the various books came to be collected into a single volume it became known as the Vulgate. Although it was influential in the Middle Ages, Erasmus' edition of the Greek NEW TESTAMENT in 1516 allowed for direct comparison and highlighted several major errors in the Latin translation.

Walsingham   An important eleventh-century shrine in Norfolk which was a replica of the Holy House in Nazareth. Although it was destroyed in 1538, Roman Catholics and Anglicans have revived the pilgrimage and today its popularity is undiminished based on a reputation for healing.

Watch Tower Bible and Tract Society   *See* JEHOVAH'S WITNESSES.

Wesley, Charles   (1707–88) The brother of John Wesley and an early Methodist. Charles received his experience of awakening to the spirit and personal salvation through the forgiveness of SINS only a few days apart from his brother John, the founder of METHODISM. Although an inspired preacher, he is particularly famous for his HYMN writing. (*See also* WESLEY, JOHN)

Wesley, John   (1703–91) The founder of METHODISM. He was ordained as a PRIEST in the CHURCH OF ENGLAND but came under the influence of the Moravians after visiting North America. The Moravians espoused a belief in personal salvation through Jesus Christ. In 1738, along with his brother Charles, he received a transforming experience. On finding the doors of the churches closed to him whenever he preached 'enthusiasm', he began a prolific ministry preaching outdoors, especially to the working classes. There are many accounts of the emotional and physical effects of his preaching on the audience. Although preferring to remain in the Church of England, he inspired a movement of lay preachers who followed in his footsteps and gradually the new DENOMINATION of Methodism evolved.

Wesleyan Methodists   *See* METHODISM.

Westminster Abbey   The present church was completed in 1540 on the site of a BENEDICTINE abbey founded in the thirteenth century. The abbey is a Royal Peculiar which means that it is independent of any DIOCESE and under the direct jurisdiction of the British monarch. It has been the site of royal coronations since William I. The Abbey's association with the state and state occasions has given it a unique place in the national life of Britain. (*See also* CHURCH OF ENGLAND, WINDSOR, ST GEORGE'S CHAPEL)

Westminster Assembly   An assembly of 121 clergymen and 30 laymen chosen to advise Parliament on the government and CREED of the national church in England after the abolition of the EPISCOPACY in 1643. (*See also* WESTMINSTER CONFESSION)

Westminster Cathedral   The nineteenth-century cathedral of the Roman Catholic Archbishop of Westminster who is the leading Roman Catholic PRIMATE in Britain.

Westminster Confession   The profession of the PRESBYTERIAN faith drawn up by the WESTMINSTER ASSEMBLY in 1646 and approved by Parliament in 1648. It remained in force until the restoration of the monarchy and the EPISCOPACY in 1660. The Confession remains the definitive statement of Presbyterian DOCTRINE for the English-speaking world.

White Friars   A name given to the CARMELITE FRIARS after their distinctive white cloaks.

White Monks   A name for the CISTERCIAN MONKS who wear a HABIT of undyed wool.

Whitsun   The feast day which celebrates the descent of the HOLY SPIRIT on to the APOSTLES at the Jewish feast of PENTECOST. Traditionally it is celebrated on a Sunday, the fiftieth day after EASTER. It is regarded as the second most important Christian feast after Easter. (*See also* GLOSSOLALIA)

Windsor, St George's Chapel   The royal CHAPEL inside Windsor Castle, one of the main residences of the British monarch who is the titular head of the CHURCH OF ENGLAND. It has the status of Royal Peculiar, a PARISH or place of worship exempt from diocesan authority and under the direct jurisdiction of the monarch. (*See also* WESTMINSTER ABBEY)

Word of God   *See* LOGOS.

World Council of Churches   An organization established in 1948, originally consisting of 145 DENOMINATIONS from 44 nations, to bring Christian denominations together to discuss matters of faith and practice. The council has no authority over individual members but is the practical expression of ECUMENISM. Today over 200 denominations participate and the organization has resulted in a closer understanding among the varieties of Christian churches. However, the 'basis' for membership that was adopted ('the World Council of Churches is a fellowship of Churches which take our Lord Jesus Christ as God and Saviour') has become a measure of Christian ORTHODOXY and has led to some Christian sects being excluded.

X

Xavier, St Francis (1506–52) One of the original JESUITS and a successful missionary. In 1534 he vowed to follow in the footsteps of Christ by spreading the GOSPEL to non-Christians. He made his headquarters in Goa, from where he travelled on missionary activities to Sri Lanka and Japan. His tomb can be found in Goa.

York   One of the oldest Christian communities in Britain and the site of the present York Minster built in the thirteenth century. While a BISHOP of York is mentioned as far back as 314 CE, the struggle for pre-eminence with CANTERBURY began in the eleventh century. It was decided by Pope Innocent VI (1352–62) that the Archbishop of Canterbury should be the leading PRIMATE in Britain, but the Archbishop of York remains the second highest PRELATE in the Church of England after the Archbishop of Canterbury.

Z

Zachariah A Jewish priest and husband of Elizabeth. He received a visitation from an angel announcing that he would have a son in his old age. Later his wife gave birth to JOHN THE BAPTIST, the prophet who foretold the coming of Jesus Christ.

Zion The name of the ancient citadel of JERUSALEM that became synonymous with the city itself. It is used by some Christian DENOMINATIONS to denote the heavenly city of God.

Zwingli, Ulrich (1484–1531) One of the key figures of the REFORMATION, although not as prominent as LUTHER or CALVIN. He initiated Protestant reform in Switzerland by rejecting the authority of the POPE, clerical celibacy and the sacrament of the MASS. He developed a symbolic interpretation of the EUCHARIST in which Christ is not considered to be actually present. The term 'Zwinglian' became associated with the belief that the Communion was only a memorial of Christ's death. (*See also* CONSUBSTANTIATION; TRANSUBSTANTIATION)

013907099

AT RISK

The term 'natural disaster' is often used to refer to natural events such as earthquakes, hurricanes or floods. However, the phrase 'natural disaster' suggests an uncritical acceptance of a deeply engrained ideological and cultural myth. *At Risk* questions this myth and argues that extreme natural events are not disasters until a vulnerable group of people is exposed.

At Risk focuses on what makes people vulnerable. Often this means analysing the links between poverty and vulnerability. But it is also important to take account of different social groups that suffer more in extreme events, including women, children, the frail and elderly, ethnic minorities, illegal immigrants, refugees and people with disabilities. Vulnerability has also been increased by global environmental change and economic globalisation – it is an irony of the 'risk society' that efforts to provide 'security' often create new risks. Fifty years of deforestation in Honduras and Nicaragua opened up the land for the export of beef, coffee, bananas and cotton. It enriched the few, but endangered the many when hurricane Mitch struck these areas in 1998. Rainfall sent denuded hillsides sliding down on villages and towns.

The new edition of *At Risk* confronts a further ten years of ever more expensive and deadly disasters since it was first published and discusses disaster not as an aberration, but as a signal failure of mainstream 'development'. Two analytical models are provided as tools for understanding vulnerability. One links remote and distant 'root causes' to 'unsafe conditions' in a 'progression of vulnerability'. The other uses the concepts of 'access' and 'livelihood' to understand why some households are more vulnerable than others. The book then concludes with strategies to create a safer world.

Ben Wisner is Visiting Research Fellow at the Development Studies Institute, London School of Economics and at the Benfield Greig Hazards Research Centre, University College London, and Affiliate Researcher with the Environmental Studies Program at Oberlin College, Ohio. **Piers Blaikie** is Professorial Fellow, School of Development Studies, University of East Anglia. **Terry Cannon** is Reader in Development Studies in the School of Humanities and at the Natural Resources Institute, both at the University of Greenwich. **Ian Davis** is Visiting Professor, Cranfield University Disaster Management Centre.

An excellent overview of the different human responses to natural hazards, dispelling the belief that little can be done to avoid the tragedies associated with natural hazards.

Gareth Jones,
Senior Lecturer in Geography,
University of Strathclyde

Paradoxically in today's world safety coexists with risk. Chronic threats, novel risks and dangerous trends ranging from new viruses to global warming crowd in on us. *At Risk* offers a rational analysis of the disasters and hazards that concern us.

Allen Perry,
Senior Lecturer in Geography,
University of Wales Swansea

At Risk has become a classic of disasters literature. Its key argument, that the analysis of disasters should not be segregated from everyday life, is an important lesson for students, researchers and practitioners.

Dr Maureen Fordham,
Senior Lecturer in Disaster Management,
University of Northumbria